Temiskaming Treasure Trails
1910 - 1915

Peter Fancy

Published by
Highway Book Shop,
Cobalt, Ontario.
P0J 1C0

ISBN 0-88954-380-1

Canadian Cataloguing in Publication Data

Fancy, Peter, 1932-

Temiskaming treasure trails

Includes bibliographical references and indexes.
Contents: v. 1. The earliest years -- v. 2. 1866-
1903 -- v. 3. 1904-1906 -- v. 4. 1907-1909 --
v. 5. 1910-1915.
ISBN 0-88954-358-5 (v. 1)
ISBN 0-88954-366-6 (v. 2)
ISBN 0-88954-370-4 (v. 3)
ISBN 0-88954-374-7 (v. 4)
ISBN 0-88954-380-1 (v. 5)

1. Timiskaming, Lake, Region (Ont. and Quebec) —
History. 2. Fur trade — Timiskaming, Lake, Region
(Ont. and Quebec) — History. I. Title.

FC2945.T44F36 1992   971.3'144   C92-094293-8
F1054.T6F36 1992

The author and publisher gratefully acknowledge the valuable assistance of the Ontario Arts Council.

CONTENTS

ILLUSTRATIONS

ACKNOWLEDGMENTS

This book relies on an increasing number of generous people for photographs and information. Thanks again to Joan Craig (Hargreaves) for her family memories. Jim Armstrong, Marvin Armstrong, Florence Dean and Bud Price spoke for Cobalt. Nora Carragher (Frisby) and Olga MacMillan (Sirr) kept adding material to the New Liskeard story. And Kathleen White (Nixon) talked of her parents just as her sister-in-law Nancy Lefebvre (White) talked of hers. And both provided photographs. In mentioning the name of her late husband Judge Jack Robinson's mother, Lillian, Julie Robinson added personality to the woman who kept operating New Liskeard's Ladies Wear store during World War 1. While husband Robert led soldiers away to Europe. The late Doug Day volunteered copies of his father Herb's *Haileyburian* editions and spoke with warm strength of what he had heard, not only from his father but also his mother whose Bradshaw parents owned a partnership share in one of Haileybury's earliest stores. So did the late Russell Murphy remember his pioneer parents. Theresa Thorniley (Joyal) spoke of her doctor father's Haileybury beginnings. Bill Grozelle sorted out his grandfather's claim staking at Kirkland Lake. And Bogart Leslie, the keenest of listeners recalled all he ever heard his parents say. From Midland, Ontario, the late John Jory and his sisters Helene Currie and Jean McFarlane could still remember walking through their father's drugstore before taking two steps down to the ice cream parlour with its round seats cushioning wire legs along the marble counter. Even further behind with its entrance off Broadway Street played the Lyric Theatre. But most memorably, the mirror of Lake Temiskaming flashed crystal morning light through the deepest summer shadows.

FOREWORD

Out of the 1910 struggles for minerals, lumber, hydro power and roads, New Ontario continues to grow. Beginning to charge the mines and mills of Cobalt, electricity from river dams on the Matabitchuan and Montreal overflows into Temiskaming towns. Noah Timmins outbids Cobalt rival, M.J. O'Brien, for the golden quartz of Porcupine. And shapes his future role in Canadian mining. Riled by insolent Nipissing Central Railway's tracks, the older T.&N.O. first scorns the trolley car antics then wins them over in a convenient marriage; branch and spur line children follow. Into Porcupine, Iroquois Falls, Elk Lake, Haileybury and New Liskeard these new T.&N.O. tracks go. While more mine, sawmill, farm sidings bristle up and down the main north-south line. And surveyors measure mileages beyond to James Bay.

Miners hoist more silver up Cobalt shafts than ever before, but its metal price goes down. Townsites rise around the discoveries of Porcupine, but forest fires level them flat. And two Englishmen find gold beside Kirkland Lake. Then an American talks of more beneath.

Cobalt's mines, Haileybury's judicial seat, New Liskeard's farms lead the northern Ontario way. From Quebec's remote Lake Temiskaming shore smoke-stack steamers trade passengers and cargoes with Ontario docks. Tugboats tow provincial logs between. Whirring along the lake's western ridge from Kerr Lake Junction, Cobalt, Mileage 104, Argentite, North Cobalt, Haileybury, Moore's Cove to New Liskeard, trolley cars ring a community bond.

Yet Tri-Town jobs will grow scarce. The lower price of silver drives smaller mines to close. A stale demand for lumber slows sawmill dust. Then a war in Europe starts. And soldiers march away, leaving Temiskaming to tougher times.

1

A BLUE AND BREEZY NOON
-1910 -

Seven years ago Noah Timmins gambled on a mineral discovery at Long Lake, five miles south of Haileybury. Now, on New Year's day, 1910, he stamps his feet warm on the Porcupine ground Benny Hollinger and Alec Gillies discovered last October. And the money he won from mining silver at the LaRose in Cobalt has given him this chance to play for gold. Three hundred and fifty thousand dollars Noah and his brother Henry have paid. And they waste no time starting a new mine.

In early December, Noah along with nephew Alphonse Paré, prospector Johnny Sauve, mining contractor Billy Cooper and his twenty-two men had set out from T.&N.O. Mileage 220 west to this Hollinger ground. Having brought two teams of horses to haul the three tons of supplies and Cobalt equipment they followed old lumber roads toward Night Hawk Lake. Through a final three feet of snow the sleighs plowed until they reached the newly frozen lake. After several trips of lightened loads across the two inch thickness of creaking ice they faced twenty further miles of solid bush between themselves and the gold site. But hacking clear a road by day, bedding down in the snow at night and singing warm an extra ration of Christmas food they have pressed forward to find Benny Hollinger and Alec Gillies' log cabin this New Year's Saturday.

Immediately Billy Cooper's men begin chopping log walls and floors for tents. And once wood stoves thaw their canvas spaces, rested miners can start stripping the discovery vein for two shafts. Alphonse Paré, though, insists they first build an assay office. His tests will then determine the drilling directions to take.

Prospectors crowd the surrounding bush. Hearing pickaxes thud against the trench's frozen soil, they snowshoe into Hollinger camp, take one look at the lengthening vein exposure and tramp away for unclaimed land to the northwest.

Yet not everyone in New Liskeard, Haileybury and Cobalt is convinced of lasting treasure here. Hardened by the boom-and-bust promises of Larder Lake, Elk Lake and Gowganda, they want eye-popping proof surface discoveries will carry rich values deep underground. Mineral deposits like those of Cobalt are not found every day, they mutter. And maybe, many admit, New Ontario's Precambrian fields mostly carry silver; why, just think of other thin gold deposits scraped away over the past few years. The Michipicoten and Goudreau discoveries of 1897 have proven more important as iron. Dan O'Connor's gold-mispickel properties two miles north of Temagami station, around Net Lake, except for iron and copper pyrites have never panned out. That government geologist William Park gave official blessing to the Mattagami River-Porcupine quartz rocks does not guarantee any depth of mining success. And remember, starting in 1900, even though government geologists, A.P. Coleman, W.G. Miller, W.E.H. Carter and E.T. Corkill wrote similar Ontario Bureau of Mines' reports on Temagami's gold region, not one of their hints has led to any profitable discovery.

Yet some fool investor, Noah Timmins first believed, had to take a Porcupine chance. Then arch-rival M.J. O'Brien of Cobalt copied his lead. After Alec Gillies and his grubstaker Jack Miller had hired Haileybury druggist A.T. Budd to sell their claims, O'Brien signed a two month deal to diamond drill the claims at the end of which time he must decide whether or not to purchase for a downpayment of $50,000 cash and later instalments of $200,000. Already M.J. O'Brien has engineer Tom Culbert sledding in the diamond drill rig.

Refusing any such deals, stubborn prospector Sandy McIntyre first wants to explore further his own property on the north side of O'Brien's option. His partner, Hans Buttner, however, for $10,000 has sold his half share to Charlie Gifford of Cobalt. A veteran of the Moose Horn operation at Elk Lake and his own mine in Cobalt's Kerr Lake region, engineer Gifford well knows neither the Timmins brothers nor M.J. O'Brien are fools: they would buy only the best insurance to protect their mining futures. Moreover, think of the sales profit from gold at twenty dollars an ounce compared to sixty some cents from silver. Jack Wilson's major gold discovery, five miles away at the south end of Porcupine Lake, has attracted its own anxious share of interested buyers. But too cautious to take the gamble, "Handsome" Charlie Denison, owner of the Buffalo Mine at Cobalt, has already shied away; despite friend Sam Singlehurst's urging otherwise. Having bought his profitable Cobalt mine for just $8,000, Denison cannot imagine stretching today's luck for fifty times that amount. Similarly nervous about their money the McCormick brothers of New York City then took a $5,000 option but have quickly dropped it. But finally Joe DeLamar, who originally helped Ellis Earle of New York finance his purchase of Nipissing Mine at Cobalt, has joined with Ambrose Monell of the International Nickel Company to pay $375,000 for an ownership share in the golden dome.

Holding claims immediately west, Clem Foster of Haileybury is content to wait for a buyer. Ever since he sold his Foster Mine at Cobalt he will not soon forget he has prospered through buying and selling mining claims. Money he has for investing, but let someone else risk the never-ending cost of ownership: he made more money out of selling his Cobalt mine than developing it. And this year since he sold the $40,000 mortgage on his lumber mill at Haileybury to banker George Bagshaw, he can afford extra time waiting for Porcupine buyers.

Sure of this new gold region's success the Ontario government creates the Porcupine Mining Division on January 27 and appoints Arthur Bruce, the assistant from Haileybury's office, as Mining Recorder. With headquarters at the townsite of Porcupine now being surveyed at the northeast corner of Porcupine Lake, he will have more than enough work sorting out the paper blizzard of claims.

Bellellen Mine, Silver Centre

At his recorder's office in Haileybury, George Smith accepts having Porcupine's work handled elsewhere but he well knows his Temiskaming Division office will still process the bulk of New Ontario miner's licences and claims. Some people now argue, though, Haileybury contributes too little to deserve this business. Take today's example that most of South Lorrain's nearby mineral region belongs to Haileyburians. Yet only Cobalt's Board of Trade offers to build a life-line winter road to the Silver Centre mines. Haileybury does defend itself: with a ready-made route available along Mines Power Company's transmission line from Matabitchuan, Cobalt can easily pay a few dollars. Bob Shillington who lives in Haileybury and is one of the syndicate owners of Silver Centre's Bellellen Mine, while also Conservative member of the provincial legislature, pleads neither the government nor Haileybury can pay the massive costs of any other roadway down the twenty-seven mile, gulley-slashed length of Lorrain township valley. Whatever, on January 27, Milton Carr with other jubilant members of Cobalt's Board of Trade bundles under fur rugs for a three hour sleigh ride to welcoming shouts at Silver Centre.

Though too far away to build a road to Silver Centre, even New Liskeard, especially since its council passed a January by-law authorizing a new fire hall and equipment, also seems to have more energy than Haileybury.

Old Fire Hall, Sharpe Street, New Liskeard

No one dares fault Cobalt's energy. Who can deny that silver town discoveries have generated all other mining activity in New Ontario? And lest anyone forget, Leonard Steenman, manager of the Genesee Mine, with Robert MacAdam, local orchestra leader and accountant for W.R. Lowery's tobacco and confectionery business, in February have the Musgrave Music Company of Toronto publish final words and music to their version of *The Cobalt Song.* Their version?

One Saturday last fall, Debbi Dolan, a nurse from St. Michael's Hospital in Toronto who had come to help fight the typhoid epidemic, was playing the Cobalt Mess piano. Hearing her sing the lines, "Oh we'll sing a little song of Rosseau/ It's the best old town that I know", Captain Jack Leckie began parodying the words into "Oh, we'll sing a little song of Cobalt/ If you don't live there it's your fault". A piano player himself, Leonard Steenman, after this evening of playful composing, picked up from where Dolan and Leckie stopped. To their first rough verse and chorus he and Robert MacAdam added final words and music. And now, Larry Stadleman

THE COBALT SONG

Written February, 1910

You may talk about your cities and all the towns you know,
With trolley cars and pavements hard and theatres where you go,
You can have your little auto and carriages so fine,—
But it's hob-nail boots and a flannel shirt in Cobalt town for mine.

Old Porcupine is a muskeg, Elk Lake a fire trap,
New Liskeard's just a country town and Haileybury's just come back;
You can buy the whole of Latchford for a nickel or a dime,—
But it's hob-nail boots and a flannel shirt in Cobalt town for mine.

Elk Lake was only a bubble, Gowganda had a few,
Old Larder Lake was just a fake, Lorrain was a whisper too,
Swastika is a rockpile, hot air is Porcupine,—
But it's hob-nail boots and a flannel shirt in Cobalt town for mine.

We've got the only Lang Street; there's blind pigs everywhere,
Old Cobalt Lake's a dirty place, there's mud all over the square,
We's got the darndest railroad, that never runs on time,—
But it's hob-nail boots and a flannel shirt in Cobalt town for mine.

We've bet our dough on hockey and swore till the air was blue,
The Cobalt stocks have emptied our socks with the dividends cut in two,
They don't get any of our money in darned old Porcupine,—
But it's hob-nail boots and a flannel shirt in Cobalt town for mine.

Credit: The Cobalt Kiwanis Club.

says, his Cobalt store cannot keep up with the demand for sheet copies. Gazing towards Silver Street at the Prospect Avenue corner where Bilsky's massive Royal Stock Exchange will soon rise, he knows people will continue singing the new melody for years to come, long after today's crowd stops foxtrotting its way up Prospect Avenue to the Cobalt Mess.

Despite its "muskeg" and "hot air", Porcupine does have gold. Having hired general manager P.A. Robbins away from Cobalt's McKinley-Darragh-Savage Mine, Noah Timmins has him sinking a shaft on Hollinger's number one vein, now exposed at surface for 900 feet. Sampling the vein's average nine foot width, Alphonse Paré assays its ore at $32.96 a ton. With such results he orders an experimental two-stamp mill to test the best method of separating gold from the rock. Meanwhile miners bag the richest highgrade for sled and rail shipment south. If manager Robbins can keep mining costs as low as the seventeen cents an ounce he achieved at his former Cobalt mine, two cents less than Noah's former LaRose Mine, Hollinger's future should be Midas-rich.

Not M.J. O'Brien's ownership of the neighbouring claims, though. After working twenty-four hours a day to finish the diamond drill test, his engineer quickly dog-sledded the core samples out to the T.&N.O. line. Yet the assays are so disappointing, O'Brien wants an extension on his two-month option to purchase. "No," say prospectors Miller and Gillies. Especially after Bob Budd tells them the Monell Syndicate, with some of its money already in Dome property, has offered $400,000 payable in $10,000 instalments every sixty days. Then after Noah Timmins bids $350,000 cash without delay, Miller and Gillies immediately sell him major control. Thanks to the McMartin brothers, Henry and Noah Timmins have sufficient money because they agreed to reunite with these former LaRose Syndicate partners on condition the fifth member, David Dunlap, also join. Restored to full strength the Syndicate is even arranging to buy prospector Clary Dixon and Tom Middleton's related claims for another quarter million dollars.

Furious, M.J. O'Brien accuses the Timmins-McMartin-Dunlap partners of destroying sane prices for all other Porcupine buyers. Yet he does not mention their possibly vengeful reason. Well do the original LaRose Mine owners remember how O'Brien gloated five years ago when the Provincial Mining Commissioner awarded him Cobalt land they so vehemently argued was theirs. Now, in final irony, O'Brien boils livid when he learns his engineer anxiously speeding the dog sled's return from Porcupine mistakenly jettisoned the most valuable quartz pieces of diamond drill core. And so lost his chance for Porcupine gold. That his son's Renfrew Millionaires hockey team has defeated the Cobalt Silver Kings in the recent National Hockey Association final does little to lower M.J. O'Brien's blood pressure.

Cobalt Mess, corner Prospect Avenue-Cobalt Street

Jack Hammell makes no mistakes. Barney McEneney, whose sciatica moved Benny Hollinger and Alec Gillies to stake him an adjoining claim for old partnership's sake, has agreed to let Jack sell the ground for a ten percent commission. Contacting Sam Cohen, manager of the Crown Reserve Mine at

Kerr Lake, Hammell offers the claim for $300,000. After Cohen's engineers spend a week picking apart its rocky outcrops, the Crown Reserve hands over $30,000 in company cash with the balance promised from future mine production. So another Cobalt company gains control of Porcupine's future.

On March 23, part of Jack Wilson's discovery property incorporates as Dome Mines Company. His Chicago grubstakers, W.S. Edwards and Dr. Jamieson, become president and vice-president. Jack Wilson, A.T. Struthers and Alex Fasken are directors. Where is the Monell-DeLamar Syndicate? Toronto lawyers, David and Alex Fasken, just as they do on the board of Nipissing Mines in Cobalt, protect this American client's privacy: and if spectacular chunks of gold keep coming out of the open pit dug into the property's massive dome of quartz, no investors need question the syndicate's apparent shyness.

Dome Mine, Porcupine

One week later, Temiskaming's Roman Catholics start excavating their own ground for a cathedral at Haileybury. Rather than out of quartz, though, its dome and spires will rise from blocks of Lake Temiskaming's limestone shore.

It will not be the only new building to lift the town's sky line. Since the four-room public school has grown as cramped as the neighbouring Roman Catholic chapel church across Marcella Street, the town has started building another eight-room one on Rorke Avenue, between Russel and Cecil streets. From two extra emergency classrooms rented this winter in a frame house on Russel Street, pupils have watched the foundation hole fill with cement and bricks begin to cover the walls. Haileybury town council has even issued further debentures for $30,000 to build a high school, $6,600 of which, on July 23 will go to Arthur Ferland for all of the lots west of Latchford

Street between Florence and Ethel. A.D. Pillar, also architect of the new public school, has completed the plans and G.F. Turney, his present contractor, will build it. Neil McAulay, appointed to supervise the high school contract, expects its last brick to slap into place by year's end. Until its students can move there, Miss A.K. McGregor will act as temporary principal in the old public school building, assisted by Miss Nellie Arthur also teaching in a second room.

Their students will soon grow used to hearing Nipissing Central trolley cars rattling down Ferguson Avenue past the old school's front windows.

With the March 9 sun rising higher in the southern sky, construction supervisor Bottinhammer has told Alex MacRae to have Paddy Quinn and his men finally ballast the rough ties anchoring 5.15 miles of standard gauge rail from Cobalt to Haileybury. By April 1, the first layer of gravel is down. Then at 4:00 o'clock this same Monday afternoon, in a sundrenched lull from late winter snowflakes, as electricity from a Wabis Falls plant surges through wire suspended between twenty-five foot high wooden poles dug every 100 feet along both sides of the track, Alex MacRae drives the first dark red, pale yellow trim painted car out of its North Cobalt barn on a trial run to Haileybury. Three of these forty-two foot long coaches equipped with air whistles and arc head lamps will carry passengers from six o'clock in the morning till eleven o'clock at night. Situated on North Cobalt's Main Street, at Stop 19 opposite Silver Avenue intersection, the 150 foot long, 60 foot wide, galvanized car barn with twenty foot high walls easily house the cars on a single track along with an extra combination baggage and passenger car. Under the same roof is the company's office and a waiting room. Now as the first Palace car glides down Ferguson Avenue carrying conductor Dan Murray, company foreman Kennet MacDonald, purchasing agent Don Jacobi and a *Cobalt Nugget* reporter towards the Vendome Hotel terminus, an electrician straddles its roof and finds the trolley's catenary rod holds firm. After hearing the car's hoot-hoot signal at the Amwell Street crossing, a pack of surprised school children chases behind. From under the few store-front awnings of early spring, people pause to stare. No thawing mud spatters them. What a change from the usual wagonwheel traffic!

One trolley line problem, however, does force Nipissing Central's associate partners Hedley Hennessy and Harry Browning on April 15 to sell their High Falls Power Company to the Cobalt Light, Power and Water Company. Last September 8 they had organized to harness the south branch of Wabis River falls to give the trolley cars direct current power. Now, though, they realize that by the time its low voltage travels the long distance from the Wabis plant to the trolley line tracks not enough electricity will be left to move all the cars. Installing a huge conductor would have raised the electrical flow but also lower the company into permanent debt. Since the Cobalt Power Company can easily convert excess alternating current from

Montreal River to direct current for the streetcars, the Wabis Falls partners gladly agree to sell their plant for its cost of construction.

On Saturday, April 30, the trolley line has more than enough power for its official opening. At thirty miles an hour cars can travel between the towns in fifteen minutes, including stops. At safer speeds, though, the company will run a half hour schedule. Starting each morning at 6:00 o'clock one car will leave North Cobalt for the Cobalt terminus at the foot of Argentite Street and another for Haileybury's Vendome Hotel. From Cobalt the track runs northeast along its private right of way then parallel to the T.&N.O. line which it crosses by overhead trestle at Argentite, continues along Cross Lake Road to North Cobalt's King Street, east on Lake View Avenue, north on Main Street to the carbarn then across another private right of way to Haileybury's Georgina Avenue, north to Blackwall Street, east to Ferguson Avenue and north to the Vendome. Of the cars' regular future runs, president Fitzpatrick says, ''We expect they will continue until Gabriel blows his horn.'' And his company will add more cars as more passengers clamour for more rides.

First official N.C.R. trolley arrives at Ferguson Avenue, Haileybury, April 30, 1910

For ten cents cash anyone can step aboard a trolley car. Soon at the company's North Cobalt office, at J.H. McDonald and Company in Cobalt and Strong's Drug Company in Haileybury a book of tickets will sell for a dollar. If you just want to travel within Haileybury's town limits, the special franchise fare is cheap at five cents. Even better will be the working man's bargain of twenty-one tickets for a dollar.

The conductor pulls an overhead cord to register each coin-box fare. As the motorman powers ahead, the door closes. And passengers soon learn the squeal of air or hand brakes can save their lives over the T.&N.O. trestle or down the slopes of Cross Lake Road and Ferguson Avenue. And they all agree the electric trolley cars sure beat the old ''Latchford Locals'' which always seemed to be forever trapped on stalled freight trains.

Yet better that was, than no service at all, New Liskeard seethes: when will Haileybury's LakeShore Road residents forsake their unmarred view of water and let the Nipissing Central Railway extend itself farther north? But why complain? the residents reply; how else could New Liskeard this May start digging up Whitewood Avenue for sewer pipes, if they permitted any such track interference. Spending $50,000 on this public system, the town will route pipes to a septic tank at Wabis River mouth and to a storm sewer directly into the river. But why, with most of these pipes buried in place by winter time, cannot Haileybury then generously agree to share a longer N.C.R. track with its northern neighbour?

Ferguson Avenue, Haileybury, 1911. Looking south from Browning Street corner

Although the main harbour port for Temiskaming Navigation Company boats, New Liskeard still lacks a government dock. And, despite this missing link, after the older company on April 6 buys control of rival Haileybury Navigation Company, New Liskeard must promise to continue cooperating with all other lake landings, especially with the loading and unloading freight schedules at Haileybury's large dock. From their sheltered Wabis River haven and the oil dock repair depot at Moore's Cove, the *Meteor, Temiskaming, Clyde, Jubilee, City of Haileybury, Ville Marie,* and *Silverland* will set out to carry passengers and freight according to time-honoured schedule— for the sake of all Temiskaming towns. Fourteen boats will continue to ply the lake. Three times a week the *Meteor*, *Temiskaming* and *Clyde* regularly steam its seventy-mile length south.

The boats are a summer life-line for Quebec's communities of North Temiskaming, Guiges and Ville Marie— helplessly stranded without railway service. Also isolated without mail and outside supplies would be Jonasons' and Bonins' Montreal and Matabitchuan river mouth farms. And the new government dock at Silver Centre townsite is the main shipping point for the inland mines of South Lorrain.

Silver Centre government dock, Steamer Jubilee arriving

During the winter anyone ambling down Haileybury's hillside streets would have seen dark beads of sleighs roll out from the Quebec shore. Heavy wool blankets over their backs, horses plodded alongside lines of small fir tree markers stretching towards Ontario. Sometimes sudden snow scurried over the lake's broad white plain, so thickly the surface blew out of sight. Yet snug inside the shelter of his shaking wooden box, the teamster gripped the reins as horses' blinkered eyes snorted out the trail of trees.

Now summertime boats will soon carry the Quebec farmers' freight of fresh meat and vegetables. Certainly the market shoppers at Cobalt Square can afford to buy. Today with Nipissing Mines banking $180,000 worth of silver each month and other operators not far behind, everyone is singing *The Cobalt Song*. Nova Scotia Mines' twenty-stamp mill is about to start; Silver Cliff's already hums.

Not only miners but also the lumbermen of Temiskaming feel like praising their prosperity. On April 30, R.C. Howie, district timber agent, reports from his New Liskeard office the past year's cut of 25,000,000 feet of pine saw logs, 15,000,000 feet of spruce saw logs and 80,000 cords of pulpwood. Adding to the year's total, settlers have sold a million railway ties and forty thousand cedar telegraph poles. With plentiful stands of bush still untouched, Fred, Bill and Wesley Shepherdson of New Liskeard are now organizing a lumber and building company outside of town in Dymond township. Moving ever up Montreal River, Booth's huge lumbering operation is cutting into east side lands a short way above Elk Lake, as far northwest as Indian Chute.

A winter sleigh ride

Picturesque Canada

Cobalt Square

Spring floods may be helping the river runs of logs but not teamsters' overland trails. Especially impossible are those into Porcupine. At least during the winter, teamsters could follow Noah Timmins' blaze marks from Kelso to around the north end of Porcupine Lake. Now, all they can do is wait until ice leaves the lakes and rivers for ferry boat rides. But will Father Paradis restore Frederick House Lake? Nothing he can do about its disappearance, Father Paradis shrugs, as he ladles full another bowl of beans at his halfway, stop-over house on Frederick House River.

In a hurry last fall to prospect his mining claim on this river, Father Paradis decided he would lower its bothersome level. Seven miles north he paddled to High Falls at the north end of Frederick House Lake. Where the fifty foot fall of water tumbled over the rocky ridge he dug a shallow ditch through the clay bank to let more water flow around the side. More water? The small cut in the fifty foot bank of clay quickly grew so broad and deep the south half of Frederick House Lake has drained away—an eighteen foot drop in water level. Even Night Hawk Lake has dropped three feet. Little did he dream, Father Paradis apologizes, that in his haste to find gold for his Temagami orphanage he could make a mistake. Since the government frowns on further settlement in Temagami Forest Reserve, Father Paradis' Sandy Inlet mission has been reduced to selling eggs to Lake Temagami's summer cottagers. Perhaps, he still prays, he might find salvation gold in Porcupine. In the meantime his halfway house covers his prospecting costs.

He would like to have copied druggist Fred Schumacher of Cincinnati who came north with money and is using it to make more. With earnings from their popular patent medicine, Pe-Ru-Na, Schumacher and his father-in-law had invested in Cobalt silver mines, then sent Shirley Cragg to find Porcupine prospects. For $22,000, Schumacher is now buying a 160 acre veteran's lot adjoining Dome Mine and another for $25,000 beside Noah Timmins' Hollinger.

That Ontario is already shaping a government townsite at the northeast corner of Porcupine Lake suggests the mineral area is more than mere speculation. Already the town's popular name is Golden City. A short distance west along the same north shore another settlement is stirring; Ma and Pa Potts, from Yorkshire, England, have found their way here to build the Shuniah Hotel. And around this log hostelry, squatters are raising other roofs over cabin walls. Everyone refers to this renegade site as Pottsville but Shuniah at its centre is the Indian word for gold.

In the business elsewhere of selling townsite lots for stores and houses, Temiskaming pioneer C.C. Farr, on May 13, charges Absalom Gibson $100 for 1,065 square feet of Haileybury lot sixty-five. Next to the promised T.&N.O. spurline on the lakeside behind O.M. Hennessy's LakeShore Road office at the foot of Probyn Street, this property will allow Gibson a storage depot for materials bound by ship for Silver Centre. Though having only recently asked, Porcupine mineowners have more than a T.&.N.O. promise to build them their own spur line and sidings.

Since February T.&N.O. engineers have been plotting the best Porcupine railway route. Meanwhile, a syndicate taken over by E.A. Wallberg has already started building an independent branch line from T.&N.O. mileage point 224 1/2 to Mattagami River.

Talk of land surveys. After years of footpath neglect, Haileybury is finally completing Meridian Avenue from Marcella Street to Main. Back in 1885, Ontario Land Surveyor Alex Niven had drawn this western boundary of Lorrain township north as a base line to measure off the seven New Ontario townships at the northwest corner of Lake Temiskaming. Yet ten years later C.C. Farr shunned its existence in his first subdivision survey of Haileybury townsite, even though the meridian pathway ran right through the centre of his street plans. Since then the town's skating rink at Amwell Street has interfered with the pathway's natural extension north; but now with fifteen feet lopped off the skating rink, Meridian Avenue edges by to complete another Main Street link with Haileybury's southern Lawlortown section.

On June 28, Sandy McIntyre also completes a straight line link with his past. Having spent the winter and spring prospecting his two Porcupine claims north of the Hollinger property, he now agrees to sell a quarter interest to Weldon Young for $300. More than enough money, he boasts, to pay for his share of drinks at Haileybury's Attorney Hotel. Later the same day after one drink too many, he sells a further eighth interest to Jim Hughes for $25. To protect their purchases both Young and Hughes insist on legal transfers which force Sandy to reveal his past. Born Alexander Oliphant in Scotland he fled his angry wife to follow footloose foreign ways of bush life in northern Canada. Safely hidden behind a red beard and the legion of prospectors searching for more Cobalt-like treasure, he must now reveal his true name and location. Maybe, though, his name will be lost in the headline news of Hollinger Gold Mines' incorporation on June 28.

Certainly people in Haileybury take little notice of Sandy McIntyre's whereabouts. Especially the Roman Catholic faithful who gather along Ferguson Avenue on July 10 to watch Bishop Latulipe lay the corner stone for their Temiskaming Cathedral. To be built of local limestone in a Romanesque design by Eugene Payette of Montreal the 168 foot long church will be 115 feet wide at its transepts and have two 142 foot high towers flanking the main east Meridian Avenue entrance. Five altars, one in each transept and three in the sanctuary will serve a seated congregation of 825. Besides this cathedral, the diocese aspires to a companion bishop's palace and convent.

Already Bishop Latulipe has the Sisters of Assumption of Nicolet operating their Convent School and Novitiate in a small house at the northeast corner of Cecil Street and Ferguson Avenue. Sister Superior St. Felicite is to have as her first novices, Sister Joseph de la Croix and Sister St. Florentine; as her first postulant, Sister Eilie de Carmel. And if Dr. Codd sells the church a part of his land north of the cathedral, the nuns could build a permanent convent there, turning over their present space to the Bishop's Palace.

Since New Liskeard provided the first place for Roman Catholic worship on the New Ontario side of Lake Temiskaming, many of its townspeople insist the Bishop's Palace should remain there beside George Taylor's house on LakeShore Road. Yet the diocese has finally chosen Haileybury, midway between the populations of New Liskeard and Cobalt, as its central site. And the bishop should be close to his cathedral.

On July 18, many of New Liskeard's Protestant women voice little Palace concern when they meet in the Presbyterian church basement to form their town's first Women's Institute. Mrs. John Sharp, Mrs. S. Hogg, Mrs. D.C. Ramsay, Mrs. D.T.K. McEwen, Mrs. Hogarth, Mrs. John Wilson, Mrs. John Reid, Miss McCamus, Mrs. A. McChesney, Mrs. William Brown and Miss Anderson elect Mrs. James Brown as president, Mrs. James Herman as vice-president and Miss E.J. Taylor as secretary-treasurer. And they promise more than idle chatter. Mrs. Earle, for example, who could not attend today's inaugural meeting, wants to help organize the town's Fall Fair. Dr. C.F. Dorsey, Dr. Fisher's new assistant, has also suggested they could help raise money to equip Lady Minto Hospital.

Grills' store, May Street, New Liskeard

Difficult it is for the people of New Liskeard to disregard latest dock additions at Haileybury. Why these alterations when the federal government has still not approved plans for a dock at New Liskeard, let alone started to build one? And why should Haileybury which stubbornly blocks railway access to its dock receive preferential treatment? Just a sensible government decision, Haileybury teases. By adding two wings to this town's deepwater dock to give 500 more feet of landing space, the government quickly explains, the lake boats can now easily load and unload a weight of passengers and freight for the three towns. Without running aground within the narrow muddy mouth of New Liskeard's port.

New Liskeard view from south, looking towards spur line and LakeShore Road intersection, Bishop's Palace and George Taylor house

From Haileybury's cement mixer tooting steam whistles sound arrogant. Laying sidewalks along Ferguson Avenue from the Attorney Hotel to the Vendome and up Main Street from the Matabanick Hotel to Georgina Avenue, Haileybury cannot resist bragging about its "superior" advantages. Furthermore, town engineer Routly is not only supervising the construction of Temiskaming's first incinerator plant at the south end of Meridian Avenue but also, to surpass the pure quality of New Liskeard's natural drinking water, is adding a chlorination plant at the pump house. About time, New Liskeard says. Digging down two feet for the new sidewalk beside Strong's drugstore, Haileybury workers have uncovered an old-time wooden box sewer. And its contents threatened to spill over Ferguson Avenue. Up on Latchford Street the rest of the town gang is hurriedly extending unbreakable water and sewer mains to the new high school.

Haileybury N.C.R. trolley tracks, Ferguson Avenue and Broadway Street corner

No one can deny the building boom in Haileybury. Back along Rorke Avenue from the half finished high school you pass the Church of England's new parish hall. When bricked complete next year it might be as large as the church itself. A short block further south at the northeast corner of Main Street, Rev. George R. Turk who succeeded Rev. Hudson in June is overseeing the building of a new Methodist church. Yet since workmen will only complete the limestone foundation by snow-time, the old Ferguson Avenue church, though too small for its present congregation of over 200 people, will have to serve again until next summer. In the same predicament until their new cathedral is built the Roman Catholic congregation across Ferguson at Marcella Street waits for more praying space when carpenters finish extending the gallery out over the centre of the old church interior for another hundred chairs. Farther south at Russel Street the new public school is now ready for September opening. John McFarlane, principal at Arnprior since 1906, has moved here to head the teaching staff. With his family for the winter he has rented a frame house at the northeast Latchford-Probyn street corner. Seven years as a teacher at Carleton Place and twelve years at Elfin have honed his sensitivity as a principal. So large does this new school building loom, George T. Smith comments to his wife Rosemary they have lost the wide-open southern view from their backyard on Blackwall Street. Haileybury's newest Fire Chief Ike Quinn can only think of how much more work his men will have, to guard so many more public buildings. Appointed caretaker of the new public school, James White assures Quinn his school furnace will never overheat nor clog with clinkers.

This August, Albert Sanderson from Orillia arrives in Haileybury to buy out James Woodworth's share in Norman Strong's drugstore. His jewellery store experience has prepared him for the gemstone wealth of Temiskaming but not for grasping why his serious arrival lightened by his own nickname of Sandy seems to have sobered Sandy McIntyre to the real business importance of selling his Porcupine claims. And now rather than accepting the price of a few drinks Sandy McIntyre signs a deal with A.J. Young, George Bagshaw and Charles Richardson for $5,000 cash and a $60,000 option for half his remaining share.

Baseball game at Farr's Park, Haileybury

Haileybury baseball game spectators
front row: Charles Richardson, Don Walkinshaw with child,
second row: Clem Foster, George (Alf) Bagshaw with cigar

On September 29, the Ontario Railway and Municipal Board finally grants the T.&N.O. permission to carry its spur line "along and across the highways of Haileybury". T.&N.O.'s strongest argument was that local industries with their total labour force of more than fifty men would otherwise have to close and move elsewhere. Since a spur line from the south is too hazardous, the single freight line through town from the north, the Board decides, "will cause very little depreciation in the value" of residential properties along LakeShore Road. And other homeowners on the hill streets above can easily see over the tops of freight cars.

Atkinsons' Main Street House - Cyril, Ted, Thyra, Fanny

View of Lake Temiskaming from Haileybury's LakeShore Road north

No time can the T.&N.O. Commission take to gloat over its apparent victory. It faces another problem. Since the Nipissing Central Railway may now also extend its trolley car line to New Liskeard, an awkward doubling of tracks must somehow find room along Haileybury's narrow LakeShore Road. More threateningly, though, the T.&N.O. could face freight competition from Nipissing Central cars. To speed its own movement of freight and passenger trains through the three towns the T.&N.O. has already started laying a second main line track from Cobalt to New Liskeard. But how profitable will this second track now be? To avoid any ugly answer, T.&N.O. may have to buy Nipissing Central's silence. Since July, Alex Fasken's Toronto law firm has been searching for a buyer. Tired of worry over balancing Nipissing Central books, company president James Fitzpatrick is eager to sell and let the larger T.&N.O. take control so he can turn to ulcer-free farming in Temiskaming.

Selling right of ways to the T.&N.O. for its extra main line track and the spur line into Haileybury, local land owners prosper. Along the T.&N.O. main line, C.C. Farr sells Usher Avenue lots 222 and 223 for $3,000. For spur line purposes, Sam Briden sells two and a half Moore's Cove acres for $500. Charles Eager sells more for $3,000. Closer to Haileybury, James Heard sells part of lot two, concession four, approximately nine lakeside bush acres, for $24. Arthur Ferland will not reveal how much money he received for the lakefront property in Block A, opposite his LakeShore Road house. But neighbour Morgan Cartwright has received $1,500 for less than an acre in front of his house on the other side of Florence Street. And Kalil Farah has received $1,000 for selling half an acre of his power station building lot at the foot of Florence Street. For his lakeshore lots seventy-one, seventy-two and seventy-three, continuing south from Arthur Ferland's, Ray Little says he pocketed $1,600. So long has Clem Foster begged for a spur line to reach his lumber mill at the foot of Blackwall Street, he might have paid some of the money himself.

Because of round-the-clock traffic over the T.&N.O.'s whole northern line the Commission has no difficulty paying for these right of ways. So profitable has railway business become, T.&N.O. revenues can easily finance the planned million and a half dollar cost of realigning heavy grades out of North Bay.

With T.&N.O.'s formal October announcement of building a branch into Porcupine, A.C. Brown and Cliff Moore of Cobalt rush north to buy land at the southwest corner of Porcupine Lake where the railway will most likely go to serve Dome Mine and the more distant Hollinger. Before winter's deep freeze they plan to map their townsite of South Porcupine, a clay covered flatness better than Cobalt's rocky rump where living problems still linger.

Only able to raise $51,000 from last year's waterworks debentures, Cobalt quickly ran out of money blasting trenches for pipe lines. But this March a thirsty Nipissing Mining Company bought the remaining $24,000 worth of debentures so Coleman township would cooperate to help form the Cobalt Water Commission composed of Mayor Lang, Reeve Ferland and Nipissing manager Hugh Park.

At this October moment, because Cobalt's Water Commission has spent the last of its pipeline construction money, its members are issuing more debentures worth $50,000. And also praying for peace between the town and Coleman mineowners. For with Lake Sasaginaga's level so low this hot summer, these mineowners organized their own Mines Water Supply Company to build a control dam and more reliable pumping station. Water rates? Both town and mineowners argue over which of them should pay less: Cobalt council claims ownership of the lake; the mineowners possess its new dam and pump house. Representing both sides the Water Commission remains mute. But with surrounding mines and mills swallowing most of the piped water, townspeople are left with scarcely a taste. And what about the promised water protection from fire and disease? they demand.

Index map showing mining properties at Cobalt

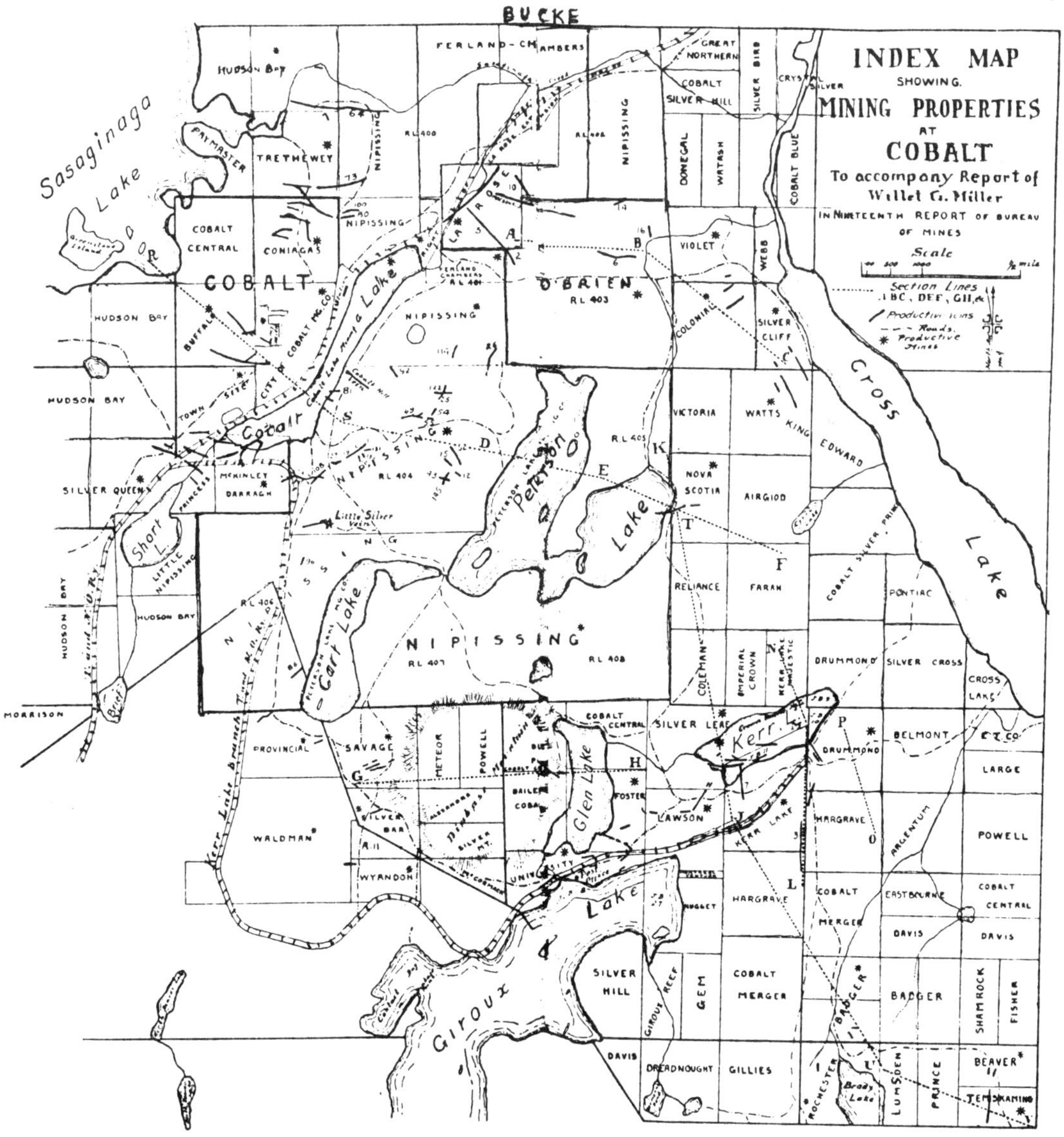

Mineowner Bilsky who, at the price of razing the Royal Bank building, is pouring cement at the southwest corner of Prospect Avenue and Silver Street for his Royal Exchange Block of offices and apartments as a fireproof example for Cobalt to follow demands the Ontario government help pay for piping more water. Until he and others can build enough commercial buildings to increase town tax revenues, some outside assistance, Bilsky urges, is owed Cobalt.

A Coleman township road

Certainly the town will have no shortage of electrical power. And since the Cobalt Power and Light Company has bought Kalil Farah's Chester Falls and High Falls plants on Wabis River, its competition should keep Mines Power Company rates low.

Away from the town's continuing water and sewage problems, Cobalt's mines are prospering as never before. Admittedly the Mine Managers' Association has withdrawn Cobalt's team from the National Hockey Association; but with only twelve games played last season, the expensive league, compared to Temiskaming baseball, has stirred little local interest. So now the mine managers are forming a four team mines' league with familiar faces from Nipissing, O'Brien, McKinley-Darragh and Cobalt Lake mines playing one another twice a week. For extra excitement Cobalt is also sponsoring a ladies' hockey team against Haileybury and New Liskeard.

What can match the excitement of last April 13, though? That Wednesday the dog Cobalt, on one of his regular visits to town, fought his final battle with O'Hearn's bull terrier. Just as Cobalt's jaws seemed to have taken the fight out of his old-time enemy, he slipped over the edge of the Lang Street embankment, a few feet north of the original Taylor hardware building site, and smashed on to the rocks below. Rushing down to the railway tracks, people found the old bulldog unable to move with hip and rib injuries. Soon after they carried him to the Colonial Saloon on Argentite Street, Bob Shillington hired a rig to take Cobalt home to his kennel bed at Arthur Slaght's in Haileybury. But too late to save his life.

McKinley-Darragh hockey team

Haileybury Baseball Champs - 1910 -

Perhaps there is too much battling excitement in Cobalt, Larry Stadleman advertises. At his stationery shop in the Nipissing Stores Block he not only offers office supplies and sporting goods but also a dollar a year membership in his public library. For an extra two cents a day why not borrow one of Stadleman's books for peaceful reading? Why totally wear and tear your body?

Leading Cobalt's companies in producing the most silver for least cost this 1910 year, Nipissing Mines has hoisted 5,590,079 silver ounces. Using ten shafts at widely separated points, the company feeds ore on to bumping tables, hand picks the highgrade and throws the remainder onto the surface dump or ships it south as lowgrade. Three hundred and sixty-seven mineral acres remain untouched, but next year the company plans to float large turbine pumps on Cobalt Lake to wash overburden off their mining ground along the eastern slopes.

McKinley-Darragh staff - mine manager McCloskey at viewer's left; accountant Charles Dean third from right

Back in 1907, Professor Miller had said even if Cobalt's veins pinch out at 200 feet, their number and richness above this level will still make the mines marvellous producers. And since most underground development has been lateral not vertical, he has been proven right. Crown Reserve's 100 foot level is so "seamed with rich leads like the veins in a man's hand" that today's dividends are averaging $100,000 per month. While local ore shoots are generally irregular the veins are long. For example, Nipissing's 64 vein at the 275 level ran barren for 400 feet before a twelve inch wide shoot of solid silver produced $800 a ton. Today, producing one tenth of the world's silver, Cobalt is the greatest and richest individual silver camp in existence. Moreover, Temiskaming and Beaver mines have altered the earliest understanding that no area mine would be worth anything unless you first found paying ore on surface. Experience now reveals wherever the diabase sill originally folded upwards, prospecting should scrutinize all rocks adjoining its fractured sides out of which mineral solutions could have burst. This year, three such veins have produced almost a third of the camp's thirty million dollars of silver: out of Crown Reserve's Carson vein miners have drilled, blasted and mucked $3,500,000 worth; out of LaRose's longest vein in the camp miners have taken $3,000,000 worth; out of Nipissing's Kendall, $2,420,000.

On more rocky ridges and treeless hills the roar of stamp mills now deafens night and day. Reducing thousands of tons of lower grade ore into silver concentrates they are producing more and more of the camp's total wealth. With its highgrade averaging 3,000 ounces to the ton, Crown Reserve so far needs no mill, only a rock crusher, jig screens and picking belt while a small smelter furnace converts the raw metal into silver bullion bars. At M.J. O'Brien's mine the electric train hauls ore muck from number six shaft over a thirty inch gauge surface track to the nearby mill. No trouble does the fifty-six horsepower motor have pulling several cars at a time. And with the spill-over richness of underground ore, no wonder it is pulling 200 cars a day. Fourteen Cobalt mills are now crushing and treating 1430 tons of lowgrade rock each day.

Crown Reserve Mine

On March 21, McKinley-Darragh-Savage Mines started shaking the south end of Cobalt Lake with twenty stamps. This same month mill superintendent G.W. Thompson also started the Temiskaming mill, two miles east. In April, Silver Cliff machinery roared up the steep west shore of Cross Lake. Besides the highgrade being blasted out of this mine's six inch wide, 3,000 silver shoots on numbers one and six veins, tons of lowergrade mill rock have been piling up in the stopes. Number one vein shoot is 1200 feet long and 200 feet deep; number six is 800 feet long and 250 feet deep. In June, the Trethewey mill started. Turning on all twenty stamps in August, Nova Scotia's mill superintendent Kirby has, in addition, the camp's first pan amalgamating plant. And like Buffalo and O'Brien mills, its final cyanide process will permit sending fine concentrates directly to bullion brokers.

Nova Scotia mine and mill

On September 1, Northern Customs Concentrates added two more stamps to increase its production to 150 tons a day. Since January, Matt Fairlie, a Queen's University graduate with ten years experience in western United States mills, has been in charge of Northern Customs plant. Operating on LaRose and City of Cobalt ores, he has pushed the plant to full capacity. Now semi-retired his predecessor, F.V. Bourne, consults. LaRose Mine has 65,000 mill rock tons on its surface dump, the biggest reserve above ground in the district. And the pile towers undisturbed. The lowgrade ore presently shipped to Northern Customs comes from residue left over after mining highgrade from the main vein's latest 154 foot long, 135 foot deep silver shoot. Also added to the shipments is some ore from number ten vein, being mined in cooperation with the Chambers-Ferland company.

Cobalt's mines now employ 6,000 men with another 2,000 involved in supporting roles. M.J. O'Brien, for example, as new owner, has extra men operating a metal foundry the Sweet brothers first built alongside the T.&N.O. tracks. Next to Deyell and Campbell's sampling plant at the north end of Cobalt Lake.

Bureau of Mines

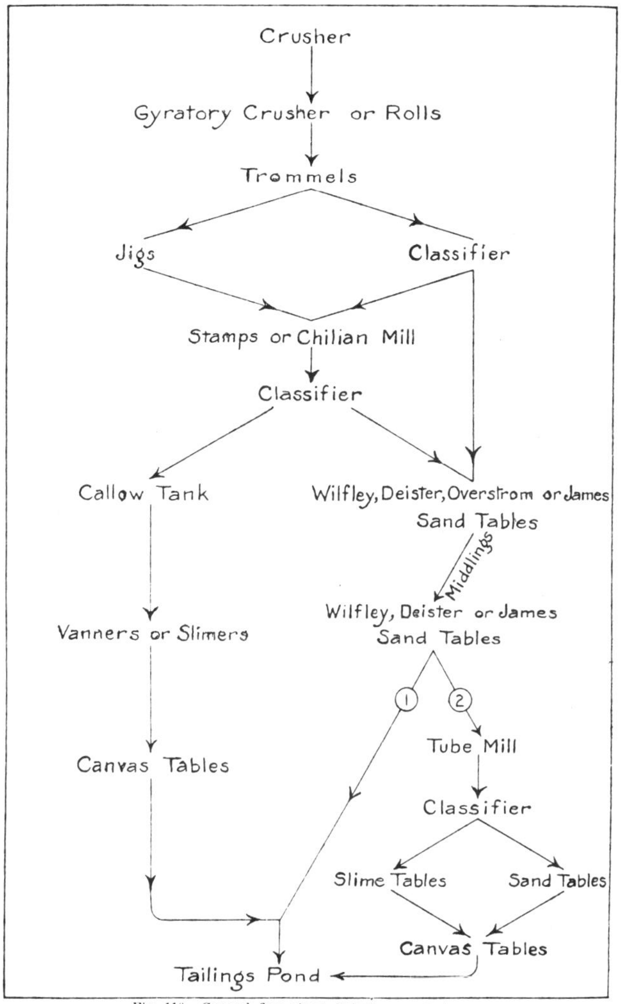

Fig. 110.—General flow sheet. Cobalt concentrators.

Out of Cobalt's tightly knotted population of 10,000 unwinds a demand for millions of dollars of equipment and materials which stimulates industrial and commercial life across Canada. Originally planned as a three times-a-week farmer's service, the T.&N.O. is now providing routine twice-a-day Pullman and dining car specials into this mining country. Three power companies have spent millions of dollars generating cheap electricity and compressed air. Nipissing Central Railway cars provide daily trolley service between Cobalt and Haileybury, whose population has doubled. Two thousand people now live in between the towns, at Argentite and North Cobalt.

Coniagas stamp mill

Campbell-Deyell Samplers & Assayers

The business life of New Liskeard steadily expands, especially financed by its Temiskaming and Hudson Bay Mining Company having paid $166 in dividends for every dollar the people of New Liskeard invested. Just ask Will Brown whose New Liskeard livery wagon squeaks more every day from heavier loads of post office mail bags. So heavy, he now wonders whether he would have had less back pain if he had stayed with his brothers Alex and James' grocery store. Maybe he should buy a permanent medical brace. For although Cobalt, Haileybury and New Liskeard prospectors have scoured the surrounding country for hundreds of miles, through Temagami, South Lorrain, Gowganda, Larder Lake, Porcupine and Abitibi regions, the end of their dividend-paying, letter-writing search is nowhere in sight.

The remoteness of their discoveries does hinder mineral developments, though. Even yet without a summer road, mineowners must still drag supplies over the Montreal River portages into Elk Lake and Gowganda.

Equally isolated, Silver Centre's mines appeal for a summer road. And since Wettlaufer Mine, this year with 199,920 silver ounces, and the Bellellen with 21,213 could become major producers, someone may soon listen.

Unloading horses for Elk Lake at Flat Rapids

Changing Montreal River boats, Flat Rapids portage

Wettlaufer Mine, Silver Centre

Miner's home and family, Silver Centre

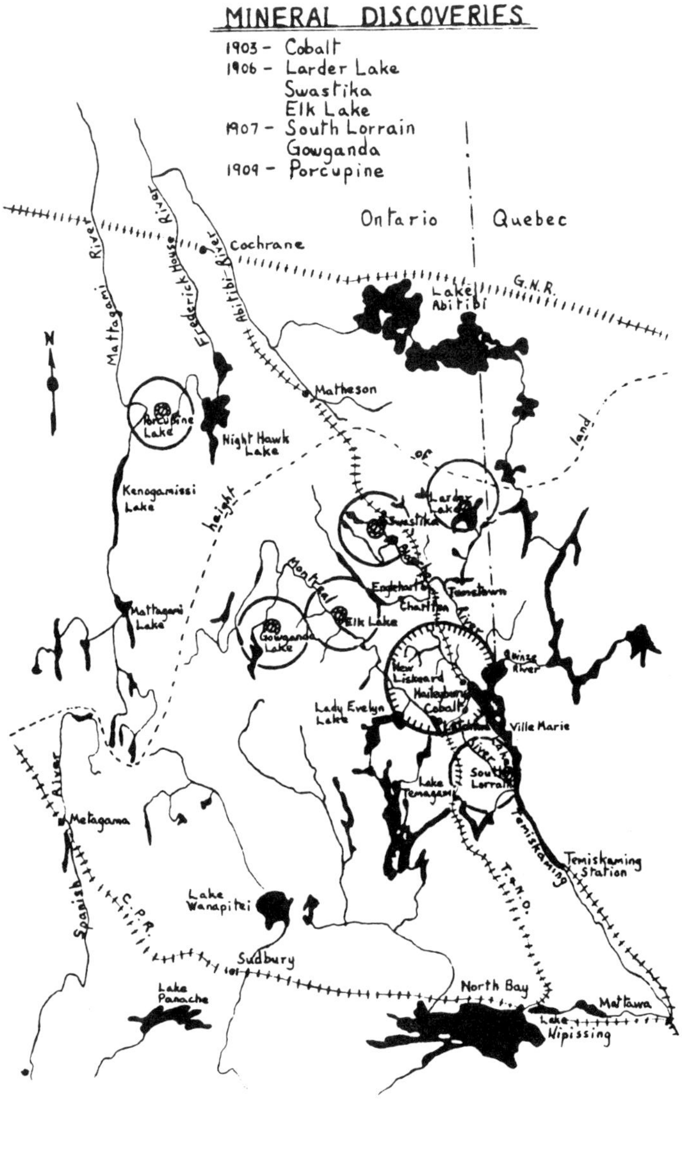

2

A RAINBOW LIGHTS UPON THE ROCK -1911-

With all mining claims around Cobalt staked and most patented, the Ontario cabinet passes an Order in Council attaching the special division of Coleman township to Temiskaming Mining Division. And effective February 1, T.A. McArthur will merge his Cobalt office with the busier Haileybury location. Firmly rooted today as Cobalt's permanent mines look forward to long lives of finding silver, local people rest easy. Always threatened, though, by the daily unexpected. Just as tragically happened on Wednesday evening, January 18, to Miss Margaret Hayes when she climbed aboard the T.&N.O. passenger train at Haileybury to wish a departing friend goodbye. After the train began moving she blindly stepped down through the hiss and billow of pumping steam, her foot slipped between the coach and station platform. Following its amputation she died in New Liskeard's Lady Minto Hospital, a week later.

Having been unable to save her from pain and shock, Dr. Fisher wonders if such sad suffering will happen father north. For, on January 1, he and Dr. Herman Moore of Haileybury signed a T.&N.O. contract "to furnish efficient medical service, and establish suitable hospital accommodation" on the Porcupine branch line being built from a point "at or near mileage 222". They have agreed to supply drugs, instruments, nurses and a fulltime doctor attending construction camp ailments. In return for this and monthly inspection trips, Doctors Fisher and Moore will receive a dollar a month payment for every workman.

Back on November 30 the T.&N.O. Commission had given final instructions for two survey parties to locate the best route for a twenty-four mile branch line from Iroquois Falls to Porcupine Lake. On December 7 the

Commission persuaded Mr. Wallberg, who had financed building Mines Power Matabitchuan River Plant, to stop work on his private rail line with a promise to pay him for the mile he had cleared to that time. Placed in charge of T.&N.O. construction, J.M. Bourke accepted Wallberg's short beginning, but waited for surveyors to point the rest of the way. Because Robert McCormick's *Chicago Tribune* newspaper had acquired the Abitibi Pulp Limit and formed the Abitibi Pulp and Paper Mill Company to develop the water power of Iroquois Falls and erect a fifteen ton-a-day pulp mill, the T.&N.O. Commission last November further agreed: as the Porcupine line pushed west another one would push six miles east to the approximate site of McCormick's mill.

Since Dr. Moore will be on twenty-four hour call over the Porcupine section, Dr. Fisher, who must remain in New Liskeard as its resident T.&N.O. doctor, has sent his assistant Dr. Dorsey to care for the Iroquois Falls' end. Having bought the Upper Ontario Steamboat Company building, already converted into balconied hospital rooms overlooking Wabis River, Dr. Fisher can perform emergency surgical chores his partners cannot handle.

Yet too late will the branch railway be, Noah Timmins knows, to replace the teams of horses hauling his latest loads of machinery for a thirty-stamp mill at Hollinger minesite. And his Porcupine Power Company could also have used help in carrying other equipment to Sandy Falls on the Mattagami River, eight miles northwest of the Hollinger. With an 800 foot long timber dam being built across the river to raise water thirteen feet, twin water wheels connected to generators will produce 12,500 volts for the mines of Porcupine. Construction superintendent H.D. Symmes expects to deliver the hydro power by July.

Not so sure whether their claim on part of lot one, concession one of Mountjoy township will need electrical power, Burr Cartwright and associates of Temiskaming Mine at Cobalt, nevertheless, have six men handsteeling a shaft to intercept the discovery vein at a depth of fifty feet.

Hollinger mining camp, Porcupine, April, 1911

Labour-saving hydro power from the Montreal-Matabitchuan rivers is spoiling miners at Cobalt. And since the Cobalt Power and Light Company is merging this February with Mines Power to form the British Canadian Power Company, machines might do even more of the miners' back-breaking work, like having 8,000 harnessed horses at your personal command. On February 1, Nipissing Mines plugged this current into its Cobalt Reduction Company, the silver camp's first highgrade mill. After testing a smaller plant for the last three years, Nipissing finally decided to spend $67,757 on this full-scale version. So now instead of bagging the handsorted highgrade and jig concentrates for shipment to a southern smelter, the company can mix its own ball mill pulp with mercury which leaches out the silver, then vaporizes under heat to leave moulded bars of refined metal.

If the McEwen brothers of New Liskeard are correct, their Wabi Iron Works plant could also be using more electricity. Doing some machine repair work for the Cobalt mines they have asked why all local stamp mill dies should come from the United States and England. Why could their Wabi plant not manufacture them? Already Matt Fairlie has agreed to test one of their sample dies in his Northern Customs concentrator. And he is serious. Over the past four years Wabi Iron Works has relied on small jobs from its New Liskeard creditors: Angus McKelvie, Tom McCamus, the Magladery brothers, Captains Brickenden and Hendry and inventor W.H. Perrin whose "Perrin Shocker" for automatically stocking grain, has yet to excite popular demand. But if the McEwens can prove their stamp die just as durable or better than the imported ones, their Wabi foundry may finally establish a steady, profitable, growing business in the mines and mills of Northern Ontario.

Northern Customs Concentrators, Cobalt

Impatient to make faster profits of his own, American Albert Freeman, on March 9, promises to pay Alfred Young, George Bagshaw and Charles Richardson $250,000 for their partnership control in Sandy McIntyre's two

Porcupine claims. Charlie Flynn who has promoted the deal insists Freeman pay $7,500 down with the balance in a series of instalments until September, of next year. Then in only one small breath of a week after signing the agreement, Freeman incorporates McIntyre Porcupine Mines. Yet a legal restriction bothers him: with part of one claim beneath Gillies Lake and part of the second beneath Aura, renamed Pearl Lake, his company must first start mining the 51.4 dry acres before it can gain title to the other 28.6 underwater ones.

In a worse predicament are Alec Gillies and Jack Miller. Ontario's restrictive Licence of Occupation law further states any land under a lake may only be claimed by someone operating the adjoining mainland property. Since two of the remaining claims they have not sold to Noah Timmins' syndicate are partly submerged under Pearl Lake and adjoin McIntyre Mine, they will have no ownership rights at all. Quickly their Toronto lawyer, Percy Parker, asks John Bickell if Cobalt's Trethewey Mine might buy these claims cheaply and fight any court battle. But instead, for $100,000 Bickell options the claims himself and on Charlie Flynn's suggestion agrees to negotiate a sale to Albert Freeman. Bickell rejects Freeman's personal $250,000 promise for the sixty-eight acres but does take $100,000 cash to recoup his option expense, $4,000 more for his legal bills and 70,000 of McIntyre's 200,000 company shares, valued at $5.00 each.

On Wednesday, April 26, the day he takes over presidency of McIntyre Porcupine, Albert Freeman sells his company the option he has just bought from John Bickell. So the company must now transfer to Bickell and his Trethewey associates the 70,000 shares. Yet on learning the company plans a public issue of 400,000 more shares, which would surely depress the market price of $5.00, Bickell demands the value of his shares fall no lower than $4.00. Or he will cancel the original sale. Freeman gives his written word.

Just yesterday the T.&N.O. branch line track reached Frederick House River, mileage 10 1/2. With the work train's temporary freight and passenger service now available to this point, Freeman prepares to travel north and speed the development of McIntyre Porcupine Mine. Probably he will never know how many labourers have to shovel four feet of snow off the entire grade to clear his steel-tracked way.

Without warm enough temperatures melting Temiskaming's great depth of snow, mineowners at Cobalt are nervously pacing. Thick ice on the Montreal and Matabitchuan rivers so slows the rise of water in storage reservoirs, the hydro plants are rationing power. How long will the shortage last? No one can guess, but already those cautious companies which have kept their old steam plants for such an emergency are now ordering coal.

A year ago, inexperienced hydro plant operators handling the new equipment caused interruptions in power but no mineowner complained since

Compressed air blow-off at Ragged Chutes, Montreal River

the new electricity cost two thirds less than coal. Some underground miners did grumble that too little oxygen in the compressed air from Ragged Chutes caused their candles to snuff out, but acetylene lamps have since solved the problem. Now, though, fewer and fewer ore shipments are leaving Cobalt; and the continued rationing of power could shut tight the mines and mills altogether.

Seemingly unconcerned are curling club members at Haileybury. Used to being shut out of the skating rink the last two winters, ever since the Meridian Avenue extension chopped part of the building away, they have travelled to New Liskeard. Now, though, they are tired of the trip. So tired, their committee of Ned Wright, Arthur Webster and John Rankin can only think of collecting money to provide curling ice next winter inside Haileybury's new market building. To construct the new building this summer, on the lakeshore side of Farr Avenue opposite the Matabanick Hotel, W.H. McLaughlin will arrange posts and beams to make room for four sheets of ice on the same floor where Bucke township and Quebec farmers will sell their summer meats and vegetables. Most impatient are the curlers to regain club membership in the International Curling Association they first joined three years ago. Even Dr. Somerville who arrived only last year to practise dentistry with Dr. Summers of New Liskeard looks forward to permanent work in Haileybury and the chance to start curling there. Not a newcomer but just as eager, M.W. Hotchkin is one of the first to contribute money for the new rink and attached clubhouse.

Maybe by next winter, mining inspector A.R. Webster says, there will be even more money available to sponsor curling in Haileybury. Already Porcupine investments have slipped cash into the pockets of local townspeople and hotel gossip persists about gold finds at Kirkland Lake. Certainly prospectors over the past five years have staked this region between Swastika and Larder Lake; yet because their trenches have never bared strong mineral traces, everyone scorns the country as "granite". On February 18, though, John Hunton and Maurice Whorley of Haileybury staked two quartz claims in Teck township—snowbanked outcrops beside a frozen creek, a mile southwest of Kirkland Lake. The two gold mines at Swastika had always made the area worth another hopeful look. And what about other disguised showings like those of Porcupine? Four days after Hunton's outcrop find, Stephen Orr of Haileybury staked three claims immediately west. Next day George Minaker staked three claims on the east side of Hunton's. Regardless of this sudden burst of activity, little serious discussion stirred at the recording office in Haileybury: "just another example of prospectors' midwinter madness". John Reamsbottom waited until April 18 when curiosity led him to stake three claims west of Minaker's up to the shore of Kirkland Lake. Two days later, C.A. McKane left his plumbing business in Haileybury long enough to stake one claim at the southwest corner of Reamsbottom's. Why? Just say I have Porcupine fever, McKane said. More likely, John Reamsbottom, Haileybury's superintendent of waterworks, had tipped off his business friend.

Haileybury waterfront, foot of Main Street, 1911

Blistering hot is the month of May throughout Temiskaming. Without rain, swamps shrivel dry and rivers trickle so low some of the powerless Cobalt mines finally do start closing. British Canadian Power Company, mineowners now urge, must think of building storage dams along the rivers. Otherwise, if the largest mines ever have to close, will the power company pay welfare wages for unemployed workers?

On May 18, when T.&N.O. steel reaches Porcupine River, mileage 17.7, the Commission's only concern is to build a bridge. And mineowners in this district care even less about the river's low level. The broad Mattagami River dam with its thirty-four foot head at Sandy Falls, eight miles north of Timmins' Landing, will soon produce plenty of electricity. Yet the brittle dry weather does worry local mineowners. From the Scottish Ontario Mine north of Porcupine Lake, where George Bannerman first discovered district gold, south to the Dome Mine and west to the Hollinger everyone eyes the tinder bush for smoke and fire. Then on Friday, May 19, sudden flames destroy all the Hollinger buildings, even the newest thirty-stamp mill just geared to begin pounding. Immediately, though, as he kicks sparks out of the black ashes, Noah Timmins orders the camp rebuilt and decides to replace the gutted mill with forty stamps capable of processing 300 tons of ore daily. With the ore dump glittering gold like a jeweller's window, he does not hesitate at the $600,000 expense.

Coniagas Mine, Nipissing's Meyer shafthouse in foreground, Cobalt, 1911

Back in Haileybury to arrange finances Noah finds free moments for an evening's pleasure at the Plaza Theatre. Here in the Amwell Street playhouse first built by his Haileybury Rink Company he listens to Alex MacLean's Rudolph Six Piece Orchestra play the latest Broadway tunes. After Irving Berlin's *Alexander's Ragtime Band* and a medley from George M. Cohen's *Get-Rich-Quick Wallingford* he feels ready to dance his way back to Porcupine.

Hardly able to afford dancing, let alone a decent meal, a quiet American visitor staying at the North Bay House on Argentite Street has stalked Cobalt Square eavesdropping on whichever conversations speak of recent gold discoveries. Losing ten cents on a trolley ride to Haileybury, he enters the mining recorder's Main Street office where the public wall map shows the latest staking in Temiskaming. What about this cluster of claims at Kirkland Lake? he asks. Only five days ago, on June 5, he reads, A. Maracle staked a claim one mile east of George Minaker's. Though the area has a bad reputation for infertile granite, Neil McAulay tells him, the prospectors are finding quartz veins. Then after a night in one of Jack Weedon's Ottawa House beds on Browning Street and a cup of coffee in the ground floor restaurant, Harry Oakes, with only $2.65 left in his pocket, catches the northbound train for Swastika. So penniless, he will later say, he had to "outrun rabbits in order to eat".

Street car, Main Street-Ferguson Avenue intersection, Haileybury

Cobalt T.&N.O. station

Educated as an engineer in Maine, Harry Oakes has prospected the Klondike, Alaska, Australia and the United States for gold. Stumbling out of Arizona's Death Valley into Cripple Creek last year, he happened to hear rumours describing northern Ontario and its mining regions. Especially the fresh gold of Porcupine. Stopping at the Bureau of Mines office in Toronto he gleaned more precise details, bought a miner's licence and train ticket for Cobalt. Learning Porcupine was thoroughly staked he narrowed his choice to the Abitibi country, then to Kirkland Lake.

Having heard its scorned granite might really be the same kind of porphyry associated with the rich gold deposits of Colorado, he arrives at Swastika, mileage 164, where he meets local bushman Melville McDougall who agrees to guide him northeast and help stake a claim for the price of a bottle. Soon they tramp their way across John Reamsbottom's claim to pitch a log lean-to near the south shore of Kirkland Lake. First Harry examines rocks along the water's edge. Then two weeks later, east of Minaker's ground, he picks up a strong quartz vein striking under the lake. Although the host rock is porphyry, the younger form of granite, no free gold shows; but he further suspects what looks like worthless pyrites may be really gold disguised in the form of tellurides—just like the geology of Cripple Creek. Knowing this ground came open in March he and McDougall, on June 21, hurriedly plant a discovery post and measure off the claim. Since the Ontario government last year transferred a further portion of Haileybury's Temiskaming Mining Division lands to broaden the Larder Lake Division, Mining Recorder J.A. Hough, on March 13, moved his Larder office to the more accessible railway line location of Matheson. So north Harry Oakes goes there to record his claim. With too few dollars to record it himself, Harry must talk Melville McDougall into paying. And to guarantee his promise to pay double the loan back, Harry has McDougall record the land in his own name. At the same time he also has McDougall sign a legal transfer which will return the claim to him as soon as he repays. Then Harry buys Melville McDougall his bottle and catches the next train to begin assessment work in Teck township.

Saturday, July 1, celebrations last into the night after the T.&N.O. branch line train makes its first regularly scheduled run to the new station at Porcupine, still called Golden City. The tracks had reached this mileage 24.1 point on June 7 and then continued 2.5 miles along the east side of the lake to South Porcupine by June 16. During the whole construction time the occasional work train hauled freight and passengers over the partly ballasted line. Slowly and carefully. Most of the ballast came from the mileage 9 1/4 pit at Barber's Bay on Frederick House Lake. At least what remained of the lake. For most of it had drained north down Father Paradis' "harmless" ditch, leaving behind a sand and clay flat with the pinched river winding through.

Interestingly, though, to uncover gravel ballast on the southeast shore of shrivelled Frederick House Lake, the steam shovel first tore away a bit of sandy ridge dividing the main body of the former lake from shallow Barber's

Bay. Its first shovelfulls spilled a stream of musket barrels, copper kettles, broken and empty brandy kegs. A short distance south several skeletons lay in shallow graves. Stopping the shovel the T.&N.O. Commission then learned the construction crew had unearthed the site of Hudson's Bay Company's ancient Frederick House trading post. During the winter of 1813 someone had murdered postmaster Alexander Belly and nine others. Burying their bodies after the snow had melted, company men from Kenogamissi House recovered what little useful material they could, then abandoned the ruins to history. Dimly remembered today the massacre still remains a mystery.

First Porcupine T.&N.O. branch line train

And more of a forgotten one when, on July 2, the people of Golden City tremble as bush fires level the surface plants of Pearl Lake Mine and Dome Extension. Except for 200 men battling the blaze, Dome Mine also would have gone. Having visited Hollinger Mine this day, Mines Minister Frank Cochrane and T.&N.O. Chairman Jake Englehart, have had to wade back through swamps around beard-smoking flames before they reached rail end at South Porcupine. How many more fires can local mines afford? they gasped. The sooner mineowners replace their spark-sputtering steam boilers with hydro power from Sandy Falls, the safer this wild country will be.

Yet before this can happen, a monster fire, no one ever imagined, on July 11 blackens the whole country. Early this Tuesday a western gale whips separate fires together over concessions one and two of Tisdale and Whitney townships. Their wall of flame falls upon the communities of Aura Lake next to Hollinger Mine, South Porcupine and Pottsville. The Vipond, Standard West Dome, Dome, Preston East Dome and North Dome mines vanish. In charge of the West Dome, Big Bob Weiss leads his wife, child and sixteen miners to the bottom of the shaft. They suffocate. Where the new headframes straddling 500 foot shafts being sunk at the Dome had been rising, where the nearly completed forty-stamp mill and a new air compressor for twelve underground drills stood yesterday, nothing remains. At South Porcupine, Jack Munroe, who helped shape Elk Lake City four years ago, organizes a bucket brigade while rescue boats from Golden City scoop up women and children. But finally darting out of mountain billows of black murk, pitchfork flames stab everyone into the wave-thrashing lake. The battering wind has also ignited Cochrane where three thousand people have fled towards Lake Commanda; leaping from the T.&N.O. station to hotels, stores and houses, the fire lights their smoke shrouded flight.

Golden City, Porcupine

By late afternoon the fire storm has thundered south into Shaw and Deloro townships. Seventy-three people are counted dead but how many others lie drowned on lake bottoms or cremated far in the bush? No one knows. But *Toronto Star* reporter Stan Nicholson has not lived to tell the news. And Mervin Stain, the former Haileybury barber cannot be found. Except for a few outlying cabins, Golden City has survived. And its residents have beaten sparks away from the railway station and freight shed. On the outskirts of South Porcupine a huge hole tangled with track rails marks the spot where a dynamite car exploded. Four T.&N.O. construction camps have been reduced to smouldering rubble. Further rail extension work the Commission approved in May to reach lot twelve, concession two of Tisdale, at Pearl Lake must now wait for at least a month.

Dome Mine's $300,000 fire loss means nothing compared to human lives. The company's 500 surviving men will have a new plant of steel, brick, concrete and galvanized roofs. And faced with the ruins of Aura Lake settlement, Noah Timmins telegraphs Fred Connell at Cobalt with an offer to buy his sand lots for a safer and flatter townsite location between Hollinger Mine and Mattagami River. At Golden City's railroad station, on July 12, he watches freight cars of clothing, food, tents, lumber and empty wooden caskets pull into the siding. Then the engine chugs away with passenger cars cradling the painful bodies of those who can be mended to the Lady Minto Hospital in New Liskeard.

Dome Mine water tank in which 57 lives were saved, July 11, 1911

Next day, dazed families poke the gray ash of South Porcupine for bits of their past. Before sudden rain drowns any remaining embers and a great puddle of black, nail-spiked mud oozes overtop their boots.

Golden City, Porcupine, 1911, Pottsville at distant right

Golden City, Porcupine

At Kirkland Lake, Harry Oakes smelled the smoke but too far away was he to learn Porcupine's fire had swept away 500 square miles of trees. Having left Swastika with as little noise as possible he had booted a bush trail to his lakeshore claim to explore further east into Lebel township. Set by hard edged experiences his mind rigidly believes the west-east length of Kirkland Lake's south bay lies along a structural weakness, a break in the Earth's Precambrian crust through which timeless minerals would have boiled upwards into his quartz vein branch. If anyone else carefully searched other rock outcroppings along this water-filled depression line, Harry thought, they should find more branch veins. And others were searching. On July 7 he met Jack Matchett, a shoemaker from Swastika, staking a claim on the southeast corner of Kirkland Lake. And three days later Dave Elliott from Haileybury staked two other claims on the west side of Reamsbottom's and McKane's claims at the opposite end of the lake. Living on lower Marcella Street beside the skating rink at Haileybury, Dave Elliott had acted on a tip from McKane and Reamsbottom, his Meridian Avenue neighbours. And so he hugged McKane's Kirkland Lake ground. Joe Grozelle, another Haileybury neighbour, followed close behind.

From a mosquito clouded distance, on July 27, Harry Oakes sees three more strangers roaming the bush around the east end of Kirkland Lake. All alone, Cliff "Swift" Burnside introduces himself. Yesterday he staked a claim beside the small lake in Lebel township; today he is staking a second one adjoining on the west, along the Teck township boundary side. And tomorrow he will finish a third claim immediately north.

Today while Burnside's axe echoes through the bush, Ed Hargreaves and Bill Wright from Haileybury are staking their own ground between Burnside's and Matchett's. Not so sure of what they are doing but knowing enough to use someone else's blaze marks as two sides of their claim, the two, thirty-six year old men do have a miner's licence, Bill's Boer War ability to suffer hardship and brother-in-law Ed's aggressive personality. Like so many others bitten by the prospecting bug they dream of royal wealth.

Since their move two years ago from Cobalt to Haileybury where Ed bought widow Marcella Lawlor's log homestead for his wife, children and a place for brother-in-law Bill to live, they have travelled each day by Latchford Local and Nipissing Central trolley to their painting jobs in Cobalt. But after listening this spring to so many Haileybury stories of the neighbouring Elliotts, Orrs, Reamsbottoms, Grozelles, Minakers, Huntons and McKanes finding gold up north near Swastika, they decided to trace their own lucky path to Kirkland Lake. No one had really found gold yet, but they all talked as if they were going to. Why not spend a week exploring, stake some claims and wait to see if they could be as valuable as everyone else's? With money saved from their last contract painting the outside walls of Northern Customs' newest concentrator addition, they would catch the Sunday train north. Then Stephen Orr drew them a map of the walking trail from Swastika station and told them to stake whatever property they could, as near the west end of Kirkland Lake as possible. George Smith's Haileybury recording office, though, revealed the only close land left open was at the east end. So this July 27, Thursday, after briefly searching for unstaked land they are tying on to Burnside's and Matchett's claims before anyone else does.

At the sunset end of this leg-weary day of measuring forty acres, Bill kindles a fire ready for his favourite rice pudding concoction while Ed leaves camp to hunt rabbit or partridge meat to roast. Northwest he heads into the shadowed trees. Stopping for a half mile rest he sits on the bump edge of a moss covered knoll. Idly picking at a patch of green, he wonders whether he should risk being lost in the dark or start backtracking to camp. Then under his hand he notices uncovered quartz and a spot of yellow. Pulling away more of the moss he sees yellow streaks etching the white quartz and suddenly realizes he has found gold. No sense shooting his gun, Bill would just think he had shot a rabbit. After replacing the moss he races south, breaking trail-marking branches along the way. When they return Bill stands mute at the sight of free gold; Ed is too excited to stay still. But they do cut a discovery post, plant it on the outcrop site, clear away some of the surrounding bush and blaze a clearly marked trail back to camp. Early next morning they start staking this claim immediately north of Matchett's. The day after they stake a third one continuing west along the north boundary of Matchett's claim and around the eastern tip of Kirkland Lake out into the water. "Three claims were all we could stake," Bill Wright would say twenty-five years later to a *Northern Miner* reporter, "because we had little more than the $30.00 required for recording."

Late Sunday night they break camp, heading west for Swastika to catch Monday's train to the mining recorder's office at Matheson. Then after the next train south to Haileybury, somebody might grubstake them to more Kirkland Lake acreage.

Better these mineral hopes than having stayed in England they both agree. Ed, a single child, had grown up in London, gone to art school until sixteen years old when his father died, then he apprenticed as a butcher at Smithfield Meat Market. After their father died in 1885 Bill and his two years younger sister Frances were placed in Sleaford, Lincolnshire boarding schools. While Frances remained in her school for ten years, Bill eventually began work on his uncle George Butler's farm supplying wholesale beef, lamb, pork and poultry to many of London's butchers. Then he joined the Royal Hussars at eighteen, went off to India, fought as a cavalryman in the Boer War and returned to England to join sister Frances' husband Ed Hargreaves in a Smithfield's butcher shop franchise at Richmond. From there Bill left to find a Veteran's Farm in Canada. And the Hargreaves' family followed. Bill may never have turned a stone on his northern farm but together he and Ed have made the first discovery of gold at Kirkland Lake, which could be worth a fortune. What to do now? Find a buyer or make a mine themselves?

Certainly people are willing to gamble money on unproven mineral property. But not everyone. Fred Schumacher, for example, has optioned one of his Porcupine veteran's lots to Archie Fuller who advises Dome Mine to buy it for $75,000. Angered by their resulting ridicule, Schumacher tells Dome mineowners if they ever change their minds in the future, expect to pay double the price.

Avoiding any ridicule over the annoying freight haulage competition which has also stalled Haileybury's spur line, the T.&N.O. Commission on June 21 did not hesitate paying David Fasken $235,483.81 for the Nipissing Central Railway franchise. Having been unable to sell the franchise for its original owner, lawyer Fasken three months before on March 13 finally bought the company himself. And while reorganizing the Mines Power Company into the Northern Ontario Light and Power Company to guarantee streetcar power he kept W.F. Stewart as land agent but appointed C.F. Beames of the former Cobalt Power company as the new Nipissing Central manager. Since Fasken's purchase, 93,111 passengers, up to the end of July, have ridden the electric trolley between Cobalt and Haileybury; so now the T.&N.O. can declare an early profit of $4,474.62. With daily receipts averaging $189.94 and more promised by the extension to New Liskeard, Nipissing Central should pay its purchase price in two years. Not a bad investment.

N.C.R. trolley terminal, Vendome Hotel, Haileybury

Too cramped within their old Georgina Avenue church, Haileybury's Presbyterians decided last year to invest in a new one. Buying another building lot up from the Browning Street church corner, they have moved the original white-washed log, frame structure there and on August 11 crowd around to watch the first stone laid in the gaping hole left behind.

Haileybury Presbyterian church and manse, 1911

This same Friday, because of mushrooming interest in the nearby Kirkland Lake area, Swastika railway station opens for freight, passengers and telegraph service. With the stationhouse south of the tracks, just west of the trestle over Blanche River, visitors can look beyond to Joe Boisvert's three-storey frame hotel, 150 feet away. Thick bush covers the background hill fringed with white birch and green poplars against a deep blue summer sky. Jimmy Doig who opened a branch of his Latchford store here last year sells drygoods and groceries around the corner from Boisvert's Hotel, next to Ed Coleman's poolroom. And since July 1, postmaster Doig sorts all local mail. Gus Mueller is ready to move his restaurant here from Haileybury. Walter Little will arrive first, though. Leaving his brother Bob and their West Road sawmill, which Jim Labine has offered to buy, Walter is moving to Swastika with a team of horses, a set of harness, a wagon and sleigh. He and partner Fred Douglas plan to start their own sawmill here. While accountant for Little's Haileybury mill, Fred has often heard his sister Lillian speak of her husband Malcolm Lang's earliest Porcupine mining adventures. So why not think of supplying timber for the Swastika mines and boards for village buildings? And if new mines develop at Kirkland Lake, as Walter's cousin Dave Elliott insists will happen, why not be ready to deliver more lumber there? Before Walter left Haileybury, F.W. Hutt, in the fuel business since 1907 who now supplies Ville Marie, Swastika and Porcupine with carload lots of Scranton coal, told him the Swastika Mining Company needed a teamster. Harnessing the only team in the area, Walter for now, at least can, earn money hauling coal a half mile from the company's railway siding to the minesite.

Once Walter finishes building a house in Swastika his wife Hanna, the Knox sister of lawyer Ed Kearney's wife Winnifred, can leave Haileybury with their two small boys, James and Arthur, in October.

Last fall, after Roza Brown quit trying to manage her husband, bakeshop and laundry at Argentite, she moved to Porcupine's Golden City. Now she, too, is about ready to live at Swastika. Preferring the company of pet animals to her lost husband, she dreams of finding her own mine, while washing laundry and cooking to raise a grubstake. Too crowded is Porcupine. But at Swastika she will have wild room to prospect. So, on August 14 when the T.&N.O. branch line station at South Porcupine opens she cannot resist the easy coach ride south to Swastika. Not any farther, though: the more frantic life of Temiskaming's older towns would knock her out of her boots.

Just last boot-knocking Saturday in the Tri-Town's Temiskaming Baseball League, the Cobalt team played at New Liskeard. Pitching against Bob Auld, Archie Burton's fast ball led New Liskeard to a 2-0 victory. Cobalt's fans would not cheer his feat, however. Even though two imports, Vansickle and Abared, from Creighton Mines did not help the silver town's team, Cobalt's manager Jake Solomon who left the bench to hit a single and double deserved being carried around the field on shouting fans' shoulders.

This August 14 Monday, the noted English amateur football team, the Corinthians, in its first appearance in Northern Ontario kicked against a select team of eleven players from the Cobalt League. Although the visitors won the game at North Cobalt by a 5-0 score, Dick Frost, the local goalkeeper from Small Heath in the English Football Association who may have been beaten five times, made several heroic, crowd-clapping saves. So foot stamping heavy were the cheers, some people feared the covered grandstand built only last year might collapse. Most of the Cobalt League players are from Britain, except for those like E. Sparling, a born Canadian who lives at North Cobalt and works at Coniagas Mine. Ever since the settlers around Milberta, Uno Park and Earlton originally started to kick a ball for inexpensive evening rests after hard days of bush-farm labour, the game has grown in Temiskaming popularity. At the end of today's game Rev. John Leigh of Cobalt, president of the league, thanked the Corinthians who in turn congratulated local players for their tireless energy.

Cobalt football team, August 14, 1911

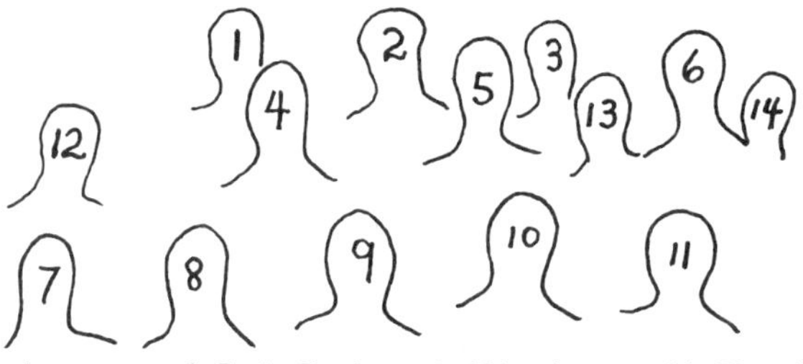

1. Percy Richards - back
2. Dick Frost - goal keeper
3. Charlie Wainwright - back
4. Harry Short - half back
5. Alex Cadman - half back
6. Jack Conlon - half back
7. E. Sparling
8. Geo. Cadman
9. Tom Wainwright
10. Fergy Cadman
11. Bert Lamble
12. Ted French - linesman
13. George White - referee
14. Charlie Pimm - trainer

Excited by the coming September 21 Federal election, northern Liberals at their August 15 convention in North Bay choose candidate Alfred Young. Only recently he sold his share of McIntyre Porcupine Mines but he still controls Northern Customs Concentrator at Cobalt. And though his Trout Lake smelter at North Bay never succeeded, he still owns his original wholesale lumbering and provisions business there. Our best candidate, his supporters declare, for just three nights ago the Conservatives again nominated another lumberman, George Gordon of Cache Bay, the present sitting member of Parliament. Why not alternate lumbermen?

Tom Longboat race, Farr's Park, August 19, 1911
From viewer's left: Tom Longboat, Alf Shrubb, Woods, Hefferon

Perhaps the most exciting Temiskaming event of this month happens on Saturday, August 19 afternoon at Haileybury's half mile racetrack. While hundreds of spectators cling to grandstand seats at Farr's Park and hug the railing around the oval course, Canada's world famous Tom Longboat strides twelve miles against three men for a $1,000 prize. Though Longboat easily won last year's run around Cobalt Lake, this time he trails the Englishman Woods, by a quarter mile. Wilting in the heat the other two men, Shrubb and Hefferon, never finish.

Forgetting these local pleasures the Temiskaming Mine Managers' Association still mourns the September 9 death of Hudson Bay Mines' manager, Jim Kinler. Checking construction of the new mill he and mine captain McMillan had been standing on a concrete pier, twenty-five feet above the cement floor. When he reached out to steady himself on a wooden scaffolding its unexpected movement toppled him backwards headfirst to the floor below. Liberal candidate Alfred Young remembers how Jim Kinler generously helped him and his partners take working control of the Silver Queen they purchased from the Temiskaming Hudson Bay Mining Company back in 1906. And often would Kinler continue to visit Young at his McKelvie Block office in New Liskeard.

Clem Foster remembers further back to that 1904 summer and fall when he was still trenching for silver at Glen Lake and Jim Kinler was encouraging Temiskaming Hudson Bay Mining Company's exploration of its long strip of claims west of Cobalt Lake. In parallel row sprouted Charlie Denison's Buffalo, Colonel Leonard's Coniagas and William Trethewey's mines. Then the Nancy-Helen and the Townsite. All these early energies blossomed into today's marvellous mining of Cobalt silver.

Foster's Main Street house (C.C. Farr's homestead to left) Haileybury

Like so many other men of Cobalt knowing local ore deposits will not last forever, Clem Foster keeps looking elsewhere. This summer he has sent prospectors into northwestern Quebec. The Pontiac Mining Company of Montreal thinks enough of that area to develop Olier and Renault's gold discovery at Lake Fortune; over a forty mile road cut through the bush from Larder Lake the company has hauled the weight of twenty stamps for a mill. When Foster heard reports of more gold showings thirty miles farther east in Bousquet township he organized his search. Now returning their canoe way in September his prospectors meet Ed Horne and Bob Bryden of Cobalt, who despite listening to a story of disappointment continue east.

Arriving at Cobalt in 1908, Ed Horne had first learned the value of minerals in the gold mines of his native Nova Scotia, then continued his education in the gold fields of United States and British Columbia. With money saved from two years of Gowganda work and thoughts sharpened from reading Federal geologist M.E. Wilson's latest report, *Larder Lake and Eastward*, he now believes there must be other northern gold deposits, similar to Porcupine's, just waiting to be found. Yet since Arctic air already freezes stillwater ponds overnight, Horne and Bryden can now travel only as far as Tremoy Lake in Rouyn township where they have enough time to pan some interesting rock on the west shore before fleeing the deepening frost of winter. Back along Pontiac Mining Company's road to Larder Lake they rush, then on to Kirkland Lake where Horne, on October 12, stakes a claim adjoining the south side of Bill Wright's lake end property. As he does, this Thursday's northwest wind swirls a veil of snowflakes over hillside spruce trees up from the bay's flattened shoreline where Kirkland Lake's water glowed cobalt blue all summer.

This first snow melts into Indian summer, though. And eight days later, taking time off from his Crawford and Gould's poolroom job in Ike

Solomon's store premises at Haileybury, Shorty Stirrup stakes two more claims for Bill Wright, immediately north of Wright and Hargreaves' quartz discovery ground. Grubstaked by Haileybury dentist Bob Robins, Wright himself had returned to Kirkland Lake on September 12 to add a single claim. Four days later Ed Hargreaves claimed another one. Seven claims Bill and Ed now control. And if the neighbouring ground northeast along the Teck-Lebel boundary had not already been recorded and held for the past five years, they would have found a way to stake this as well.

Close enough to Swastika are Kirkland Lake claims for prospectors to sled in supplies for winter work. A happy accident, mine developers would say. But compare the present-day pains of Elk Lake and Gowganda. Desperate for a railway connection to the main line of Temiskaming, their mineowners led a May delegation to Queen's Park to push the summer beginning of a branch line. But disappointment now chills them as the government engineer's report in November condemns any Charlton extension. Through country rough and rocky, without "agricultural merit", a 17.8 mile line to Elk Lake would never recover its $570,000 cost, maybe not even the additional $65,000 cost of bridging Montreal River. Why then not extend the newly completed Porcupine line due south over the height of land into Gowganda district? The summer survey report on this possibility will be ready next month. Wait for it.

Speaking from Hudson Bay Mining Company's headoffice at New Liskeard, President George Taylor deplores government indecision. Developing a silver property near Hanging Stone Lake, south of Gowganda Lake, his company has had to drag two fifty horsepower boilers, another twelve horsepower one, a three drill compressor and hoist across V-cut ravines, through quicksand swamps and an endless maze of trees. In forty degree below zero temperatures and snow so deep horses sink up to their necks, winter haulage is little better. Sinking a two compartment shaft over 100 feet, the company is impatient to start drifting on the vein. And make enough money to pay its bills. Yet hauling any silver highgrade for distant sale may take so long, creditors cannot afford to wait. A government railroad would help prevent such failure.

Relying on its Montreal River shipping business, however, Latchford fears any branch rail line into Elk Lake. Already suffering from fires, this summer and last, burning down their wooden stores, townsite businessmen know Latchford's loss of river-traffic trade would be a final killing blow. Just as fearful, though, are the isolated businessmen of Elk Lake and Gowganda who combined with surrounding mineowners also want to stay alive.

No such problem panics Porcupine. Moreover, by October, Noah Timmins has seen the first of the residential and business lots auctioned to excited bidders at his new townsite between Hollinger Mine and Mattagami River. The $500 to $1,500 prices remind him of Cobalt's similar sale six years ago. Now, though, to avoid Cobalt's birth pains, he will maintain tight control of the delivery. On the town's main Third Avenue thoroughfare he will build the Goldfields Hotel. Hollinger Mine will build a solid row of weatherproof houses for its miners. To bring their families, the branch line rail extension from South Porcupine should reach Third Avenue by year's end. And since the September 17 closing of Kelso station with the rerouting of platform service through Iroquois Falls' junction station, no longer will shunting mix-ups confuse freight or passengers. Noah Timmins vows, unlike the T.&N.O. Commission's ownership of Cobalt, he will never abandon his town during its infancy.

Having grown during the past decade, thanks to precocious Cobalt, the older towns of New Liskeard and Haileybury are squabbling over which should become the judicial centre of Temiskaming District. On November 24, the *New Liskeard Speaker* says

Choose New Liskeard the district town. Cobalt may continue to be a permanent town, and Haileybury may continue to be its suburb, but there is no doubt about the future of the agricultural town of New Liskeard. Mines may become exhausted but good farming land does not....
The district seat should be placed in the town having the brightest prospects for permanency. This being the case New Liskeard should be chosen.

Joe Brown farm, south half lot 2, con. 2, Chamberlain township

Haileybury may have almost completed building its high school but Miss Isabella Dobbie, replacing Mr. Sparks as principal, says New Liskeard's continuation school will do just as thorough, maybe even better, an educational job. Despite her admission it cannot teach senior forms. And consider New Liskeard's completed library on Whitewood Avenue corner, filling the continuation school's frontyard. Made of limestone from Mann's Island and paid for by last year's gift from the Carnegie Foundation, this one-of-a-kind New Ontario book centre opened on July 3. Charles Byam who was on the building committee says Mrs. Edith Gold, librarian and secretary for the past two years spending three and a half hours each afternoon and two and a half hours each evening, now has a full time job. So many people are using the library, Capling and Hickling's ladies and children's wear store directly across Whitewood Avenue complains of losing customers.

Also consider the growing strength of New Liskeard industry: since the Wabi Iron Works steel dies tested in Northern Customs Concentrator plant have outlasted all foreign ones, mill manager Matt Fairlie and consultant Frank Bourne have asked whether the New Liskeard company can produce stamp dies in quantity. And when the McEwen brothers replied "Yes" if only they had a larger factory, the Cobalt company after checking Wabi's balance sheet and Percy Craven's audit has promised to help. In the meantime, Northern Customs wants as many dies as the Wabi plant can produce. And wait until all the other mills of Cobalt and growing Porcupine start placing similar orders.

If anyone needs proof of New Liskeard's agricultural strength, consider the success of this year's special T.&N.O. Demonstration Car which Ontario's Department of Agriculture sponsored to tour the province publicizing the farms of New Ontario. Even the far north.

Along with its exploratory survey of the lowlands between Cochrane and James Bay for a possible ocean harbour site at Moose Factory, the T.&N.O. also wants to open up the larger 150 mile wide clay belt extending westward from Quebec border for 350 miles with the National Transcontinental Railway passing through its middle. Already in response to southern publicity a flow of letters into the Crown Lands office at New Liskeard started in July and still continues. But whether dissatisfied with land in outlying Temiskaming townships or a place to live in New Liskeard itself, the farmers of southern Ontario must bide their time before moving farther north. They may easily decide to stay near Lake Temiskaming.

Not in Cobalt, though, where avalanche rock dumps are now squeezing the townspeople into even narrower lots. But not aspiring to the additional prestige of District judicial seat, Cobalt is content to live on mining.

Too far away from the three largest Temiskaming towns is the choice of Latchford and Englehart as District seats. Yet North Cobalt is centrally located. And housing some 2,000 people, its flat expansive townsite including neighbouring Argentite could easily accommodate judicial buildings. The Nipissing Central trolley cars running along the 100 foot width of Lakeview Avenue and Main Street start and end here each day. And with the line's extension to New Liskeard next year, North Cobalt's electric trolleys will knit all the major towns together. Although the Nipissing Central conductors and motormen signed an October 14 petition for a raise in wages to $3.00 a day for experienced men and $2.75 for beginners which seemed to threaten local harmony they have since settled for 25 cents less. In final favour of North

Cobalt's choice, anyone travelling the main T.&N.O. line can make direct trolley car connection at the townsite's railway station.

Five years ago, M.J. Ferguson moved his post office to North Cobalt from its Market Street location in Argentite. Since steamships no longer carried supplies to the Kerr Lake mines near the south end of Cross Lake, Port of Cobalt's Mill Creek dock area quickly filled with logs. Today, rather than sluice them past the dam down to Lake Temiskaming, foreman Felix Lacarte has most of them pike-poled ashore into McCamus and McKelvie's creekside mill. Cheaper it is to saw Bucke township trees here and ship T.&N.O. boxcars of lumber north to storage yards at New Liskeard. In the more populated townsite of North Cobalt, the post office first occupied one half of Lillie's General Store at the corner of LakeView Avenue and Cross Lake Road. But now Charles Courtemanche, having just replaced Ferguson as postmaster in June, has built a large postal building on LakeView Avenue, west of Lillie's.

That Haileybury's population now exceeds New Liskeard's; that its hotels swell full from Cobalt business; that its enlarged steamship wharf handles much of Lake Temiskaming's freight, and more, once Haileybury's railway spur is complete; that Foster's Mill, the Haileybury Brick Company, the Explosives factory are just a few of the town's businesses suggests Haileybury is equal to New Liskeard in the race for District judicial seat.

North Cobalt T.&N.O. station

Keep the race fair, though. That Temiskaming's member of the Conservative government at Queen's Park lives in Haileybury, the *New Liskeard Speaker* warns, must not bias the provincial Cabinet's final decision. But when, on December 25, the Roman Catholic diocese of Temiskaming opens its Cathedral doors at Haileybury, the *Haileyburian* mocks its New Liskeard rival, saying the Ontario government will surely have as much good sense as the Roman Catholics in choosing central Haileybury.

Rather than choose sides, Holy Cross Cathedral choir prefers harmonizing hymns. So, L. Jodouin conducts Charles Day, Joe Brisebois, Frank Philips, Ernest Phelps, J. Peloquin, J.W. McDougall, L.H. Ferland along with 118 men and women's voices in their church's Christmas birthday. The choir can look forward to Sister St. Clair of Assumption Convent accompanying them on the organ next year as construction started on the Haileybury convent in September. For now, the orchestra of Dr. Codd, W. McCurdy, H. Poppleton, A.B. Smith and H. Trudel provides instrumental music.

Up the T.&N.O. line, Uno Park, Thornloe, Heaslip, Dane and Swastika have no illusions about being appointed the district town of Temiskaming. But Walter Little's family in Swastika wishes at least one church bell could remind them of Christmases past in Haileybury. Nevertheless they can gather in the newly built Methodist church where Hanna Little will play the harmonium. And since, on December 14, the residents of Swastika successfully petitioned for a school section, her sons will soon have a week-day school to attend. To cheer village loneliness, Joe Boisvert now invites everyone to share singing carols and opening gifts in his Swastika hotel. And so the Littles again feel the social warmth of pioneer Temiskaming days.

Assumption Convent being built, Haileybury,
Nellie Codd & daughter Dorothy in foreground

Pioneer days more often forgotten now in the rush of mining wealth. But how could Cobalt this year, having produced a record 31 1/2 million ounces of silver at a market price of 53 cents, keep its mind on anything else? Even its cobalt ore selling at 72 cents a pound may soon be in profitable demand. Mr. Elwood Haynes of the Haynes Automobile company in Kokomo, Indiana, is working on a cobalt and chromium alloy to resist corrosion and harden metal cutting tools. His stellite, he says, can give small knives an edge comparable to tempered steel. At present, though, only 300 to 500 tons of cobalt oxide is used each year in France, England and Germany to colour fine chinaware blue. And out of a total production this year of 1,098 tons, Cobalt's mines have sold only 379 tons of $54,699 worth. Now stockpiled, the rest is practically waste.

TABLE SHOWING SILVER PRODUCTION IN 1911

Company	Troy Ounces Shipped
Nipissing	4,627,043
La Rose	4,090,156
Crown Reserve	3,430,902
Coniagas	3,273,465
McKinley-Darragh-Savage	2,551,885
Kerr Lake	2,238,353
Buffalo	1,644,245
O'Brien	1,397,546
Temiskaming	1,162,317
Hudson Bay	1,067,667
Wettlaufer-Lorrain	925,017
Beaver	888,876
Cobalt Townsite	834,949
Trethewey	716,464
Cobalt Lake	626,044
Miller Lake-O'Brien	338,000
Right of Way	289,718

Cobalt silver vein, Temiskaming Mine

No surprise is this record year of silver production to Professor Willet Miller. Even after first visiting the Long Lake discovery in the fall of 1903, he reported shortly after in the December 10 edition of the *Engineering and Mining Journal*

The ore is undoubtedly very rich containing values in nickel, cobalt, silver, and arsenic, and a comparatively small vein could be worked at a handsome profit.

Cashing their latest dividend cheques, shareholders in Cobalt's major mines agree with Professor Miller's original words.

COBALT MINING DIVIDEND PAYMENTS

Name of Company.	Date of Incorporation.	Authorized Capital.	Capital Stock issued.	Par value per share.	Amount of Dividends and Bonuses declared to end of 1911.
		$	$	$	$ c.
Beaver Consolidated Mines, Limited	Mar. 5, 1907	2,000,000	2,000,000	1.00	170,000 00
Buffalo Mines, Limited	April 27, 1906	1,000,000	1,000,000	1.00	1,377,000 00
City of Cobalt Mining Company, Limited	Oct. 5, 1906 Jan. 7, 1909	500,000 1,500,000	1,500,000	1.00	139,312 42
Cobalt Central Mines Company	Dec. 13, 1906	5,000,000	5,000,000	1.00	192,846 00
Cobalt Lake Mining Company, Limited	Dec. 22, 1906	†5,000,000	3,929,166	1.00	....
Cobalt Silver Queen, Limited	April 1, 1906	1,500,000	1,500,000	1.00	315,000 00
Cobalt Townsite Mining Co., Limited	May 6, 1906	100,000	45,011	1.00	125,000 00
Coniagas Mines, Limited	Nov. 21, 1906	4,000,000	4,000,000	5.00	2,840,000 00
Crown Reserve Mining Company, Limited	Jan. 16, 1907	2,000,000	1,999,957	1.00	3,714,509 40
Foster Cobalt Mining Company, Limited	Feb. 14, 1906	1,000,000	915,588	1.00	45,000 00
Kerr Lake Mining Company	Aug. 9, 1905	3,000,000	3,000,000	5.00	3,940,000 00
La Rose Consolidated Mines Company	Feb. 21, 1907	7,500,000	7,493,135	5.00	2,672,000 00
McKinley-Darragh-Savage Mines of Cobalt, Limited	April 9, 1906	2,500,000	2,247,692	1.00	2,156,721 38
Nipissing Mines Company	Dec. 16, 1904	6,000,000	6,000,000	5.00	8,325,797 25
Right of Way Mining Company, Limited	July 13, 1906	500,000	500,000	1.00	324,643 93
The Right of Way Mines, Limited	Sept. 11, 1909	2,000,000	1,685,500	1.00	202,260 00
Temiskaming and Hudson Bay Mining Company, Limited	July 29, 1903	25,000	7,761	1.00	1,521,156 00
The Hudson Bay Mines, Limited	July 16, 1909	3,500,000	3,200,050	5.00	394,903 42
Temiskaming Mining Company, Limited	Nov. 16, 1906 Jan. 1, 1908	2,500,000	2,500,000	1.00	1,009,156 00
Trethewey Silver Cobalt Mine, Limited	May 30, 1906 June 1, 1911	1,000,000 2,000,000	1,000,000	1.00	761,998 50
Wettlaufer Lorrain Silver Mines, Limited	Nov. 30, 1908	1,500,000	1,416,590	1.00	283,318 00

Although it now appears Porcupine gold may someday eclipse Cobalt's earnings, people should someday remember the quick profits of Cobalt's mines made Porcupine development possible. This was part of Malcolm Lang's Liberal message on December 11 when he won the new seat for Cochrane South in the provincial legislature. Yet even though the year-end merger of Cobalt Power Company and Cobalt Hydraulic Company's two Montreal River plants under the name of Northern Ontario Light and Power Company should remind today's people of Temiskaming to thank Cobalt, people should also remember New Liskeard first harnessed New Ontario's hydro power.

According to lawyer Fred Elliott, known as "Judge" Elliott because his expert knowledge of mining law so often proves correct, not even gold can eclipse a man. Living with a weakness for whiskey at Haileybury's Vendome Hotel he regularly "repairs to the bar" after his evening meal. One autumn night while gazing out the hotel window at the moon over Lake Temiskaming, he said, "Alright, you are full tonight but I am full every night."

Two years ago, Fred Elliott was defending a mining claim case in North Bay court. After listening at length to what he considered too fine an argument, the presiding judge finally said, "Now, Mr. Elliott, you are just wasting my time. I have already decided, so what you are saying is just going in one ear and out the other."

Quickly Fred Elliott said, "I know how it is, your Honour, nothing there to stop it."

Down exploded the judge's gavel, "Mr. Elliott, you will apologize to this court or you will never plead another case in my court and I'll have you disbarred."

After Elliott meekly apologized, the judge told him to proceed with his case. "I'm through, your Honour."

"Case dismissed!" the judge declared.

"Thank you, your Honour," Elliott replied, "and I also want to thank you for accepting my apology. You see, your Honour, it was just a vagrant thought that ran through my mind and I was unfortunate enough to put it into words."

A summer's relaxation - Old Mission picnic, Lake Temiskaming

Cobalt from south side of Cobalt Lake

3
WAVES LEAPING GREEN
-1912 -

Though incorporating as an independent town on January 1, 1912, Timmins acknowledges most of its money and miners come from Cobalt. A natural happening in the world of mining where owners are always planning a further move to restock their mineral shelves with prospectors' fresh discoveries. And they ever wait for prospectors to search.

Staying at John Weedon's boarding house on Browning Street in Haileybury, Harry Oakes on Sunday, January 7, takes the train north to Swastika. His family in Maine has loaned him enough money to pay this winter's bills and after another reading of latest registrations in the Mining Recorder's office, he is on his coach ticket way to stake more claims at Kirkland Lake. He needs help, though. And when he meets the four Tough brothers, George, Tom, Bob and Jack at Boisvert's Hotel, he finds it. Besides clearing their farmland near Charlton and spending the last four winters hauling equipment and supplies into the mines of Elk Lake and Gowganda for men like Clem Foster, they have turned their hand to prospecting. Yet now, though they do have their miner's licences intact, they have been looking for some winter place to make money cutting logs. But Harry Oakes' talk of sharing five Kirkland Lake gold claims in exchange for their help is intriguing. And most exciting. Since the claims open for restaking in a few hours time—at midnight.

Granted extensions for assessment work on these five Teck and Lebel township claims since 1906, the Burrow brothers have run out of ownership excuses. So their forfeited land will next belong to whoever stakes it first. After listening to Harry's fist-pounding stories of prospecting trips around the world which have led here to possible glories at Kirkland Lake, the Tough brothers are ready to follow. Yet only Tom and George choose to go; the others want to protect their lumber business.

Walking the beaten path to Lucky Cross Mine, Harry and his new partners continue north along the frozen line of Amikougami Creek. Snowshoes lift them over four foot drifts but the air is flesh-cringing cold. The dim glow of candles flickering inside perforated tin can holders barely shadows their deep tracks. Nevertheless, stars crackle clear in the black sky where the Big Dipper points Polaris' compass path and their five mile slog through silent bush. After veering east onto Stephen Orr's property, they have to lift their legs hobbled by two and three pairs of pants a few hundred more yards onto the hard crust of Kirkland Lake, then towards sentinel trees looming along the far side, where Wright, Hargreaves and Burnside staked last July. By 3:00 a.m., the fifty-six below zero temperature has slowed their stride. George Tough will later remember "I think Oakes had on about five pair of pants and we had a few pairs, too." With no time to light a fire, boil tea or chew hard tack, they quickly move to locate and replace the old claim posts.

On Tom Tough's licence they measure off the first two claims in Teck township then on Harry's they stake the final three east around the near end of a smaller lake in Lebel. While a faint glow of orange begins to creep up the eastern sky, with their job done they kindle a campfire. Then Bill Wright sees its thin plume of smoke. And mutters over a mug of their tea about his and young Stan Fleming's late arrival. Bill had promised Stanley, an Englishman from Tunbridge Wells whom he and Ed Hargreaves had protectively befriended during their early Cobalt days, a share in staking this latest opportunity. But now all Bill is left to talk about is his and Ed's quartz outcrop find last July. Amazed by this story of beginner's luck the Toughs quickly agree with Harry to spend the week searching for similar humps of rock before they leave to record their claims at Matheson. And return in February. Three days later, wandering still father east, George Tough brushes off a quartz vein outcrop speckled yellow and stakes his own separate claim.

Back at Swastika, T.&N.O. station agent W. Brennan says if Kirkland Lake prospects prove valuable the area might some day have its own branch rail line. Anderson and McQuire have already opened a Swastika assay office. And P.J. Finlan from Cobalt has building lots for sale in partner Sam Maddin's subdivision on the south Otto Lake side of the T.&N.O. tracks.

Certainly rich discoveries of gold have made the branch line possible at Porcupine where the rail extension now stretches even further west out of South Porcupine. On February 12, freight traffic opens to Schumacher, mileage point 31.7, and to Timmins, mileage point 33.2. By March 11, both stations will have passenger train service; by July 8, railway and commercial telegraph wires.

With a branch line into Elk Lake finally approved, the T.&N.O. Commission has hopes, as well, for faded mining prospects. And on February 24, the Commission calls for construction tenders, to close on March 20. Last year's November survey has confirmed the best route is southwest and west from Earlton, crossing Montreal River, just above Mountain Lake, then up river to Elk Lake townsite. This route may be eleven miles longer than the old Charlton winter sleigh trail, but with easier curves and grades the construction cost is the same. Furthermore, contrasted to Charlton's rocky way, the Earlton line will provide farm access to more flat lying clay lands reaching west. And with the tracks bridging Montreal River, the railway end will stand poised to push even farther west to Gowganda, if future mining beckons. On to mineral lands scarcely scratched by our picks, local prospectors say.

Bitter, though, is New Liskeard over the subject of branch rail lines. In March, the town's Wabi Iron Works, its experimental dies still outlasting the foreign ones presently used in Cobalt's stamp mills, has to decide whether to move its factory from the Wabis River steamship supply location closer to a T.&N.O. main line track connection with Cobalt. Mine and mill owners there are clamouring for them to do so. Then after Colonel Leonard of the Coniagas, M.J. O'Brien of the O'Brien, Norman Fisher of the Temiskaming, Alfred Young and Frank Bourne of Northern Customs Concentrators agree to invest $5,000 apiece to enlarge Wabi's stamp-making capacity, the New Liskeard company knows it must move from expensive wagon-delivery isolation at the lake end of Whitewood Avenue, west to the railway. With Alfred Young as president and Frank Bourne managing director, works manager Hugh McEwen will supervise his reorganized company's new factory across the main T.&N.O. tracks on the south side of Broadwood Avenue.

New Liskeard T.&N.O. station

No such move would be necessary if New Liskeard had its own completed railway spur line, the town complains. Paralyzed between the federal government's empty promise to build a Wabis River dock and the T.&N.O.'s few feet of aborted spur, New Liskeard businessmen are rigid with frustration. Now the Wabi Iron Works must move, but what about the ships it used to service? And the farmers who rely on these ships? A spur line would have allowed Wabi Iron Works to stay near the lake, while Blanche River and Quebec farmers enjoyed the additional advantage of directly loading their agricultural produce aboard railway cars.

Persuade the federal government to build a dock and we will complete your spur line connection, T.&N.O. commissioners say. Only then can boxcars roll in and out of your town carrying the tonnages of timber, grain and meat so many horses and wagons must slowly haul through today's streets. But, meanwhile, you must accept Wabi Iron Works' move to a higher and drier site. Consider each springtime when the factory ground becomes a muddy mire from flooding lake water. And forced to find space outside the factory walls to fill and pour ladles holding 200 pounds of molten metal, how often have workmen suffered burns from steaming mud or water the dripping metal splashed up on to their arms and faces? Furthermore, how many hundreds of tons of rock would be required to give this soggy area a firm foundation?

Piché's Point wharf, Lake Temiskaming

All the time New Liskeard has been begging Ottawa, the government dock at Haileybury has grown even larger and steamships have tied up to new ones at Silver Centre and Piché's Point. Favouritism?

Why should the people of Haileybury who refused a spur line through their town deserve special dock favours, when New Liskeard does not even have one? Avoiding a direct answer, Haileybury mentions since the T.&N.O. last year bought the Nipissing Central Railway line, its town council has now generously agreed to a lakeshore spur line and also an extension of the Nipissing Central trolley to New Liskeard. Nonsense, New Liskeard says: because the Ontario Railway and Municipal Board in last year's decision gave the T.&N.O. absolute right to build both, Haileybury has had no choice.

While not part of this debate, Dr. Codd of Haileybury shows how the two towns, despite their angry quarrels, do work in common northern cause. Hitching a last-minute cutter ride from Dunseath's Livery, only two blocks south of his Meridian Avenue front door, Dr. Codd races to the railway station for a mid-day trip to Iroquois Falls. As Temiskaming's coroner he must conduct an inquest to determine the "accidental death" of T.&N.O. brakeman Charles La Mourie who fell under a shunting train at 8:50 a.m., March 5; although sped by special train to New Liskeard's Lady Minto Hospital, he died the same afternoon.

But how can the two towns create a living co-operation warmer than sharing the medical misery of fatal accidents? Perhaps their frequent exchange of jealous insults over who should best share in the riches of Cobalt has soured any present chance for friendship. And for another mistaken moment of instant pleasure, Haileybury is again too busy to care.

J.A. Dunseath's Livery Barn - Meridian Avenue, Haileybury, 1912

Friday, March 8, at Haileybury the Whitby girls' southern Ontario hockey team, plays Haileybury's Northern Ontario champions. With adult admission priced at 75 cents and the game to start at 8:15 p.m. a thousand people jam the rink waiting for "God Save The King" to end, for referees J. Smith of Whitby and Teddy Oke of Haileybury to drop the puck. Then, except for fifteen minutes before the end of the game, Haileybury dominates the contest by a 3 to 1 score. Miss McParland in goal was able to rest most of the evening as Haileybury defensive stars, Miss Jamieson, at point, and Miss Powers, at cover, led the play up ice to score all three goals. Haileybury forwards Mrs. Ferguson, at centre, Miss McKay, right wing and Miss Noonan, left wing, checked Whitby's team to a standstill. But only until Miss Blanchard's lone goal, scored after her team-mate Miss Smith fell to the ice when hit in the face and Miss Noonan left the game to keep both sides equal, seemed to strengthen the visitors. With too few minutes left to play.

Captain Leckie whose engineering skills helped many Cobalt mines' early beginnings has decided he has no local time left to play. So on Saturday night his fellow members gather at the Cobalt Mess to present him with a gold watch. Except for George Ross, he is the only charter member remaining in town. After the banquet supper the party moves to Hugh Park's house where Captain Leckie and Eddie Holland entertain with their songs. Tomorrow Captain Leckie will wish a last farewell to his many friends still standing at the station as the train starts him on a journey to new days in British Columbia.

For a dedication service, on Sunday, March 10, Haileybury's Methodists gather in their new church's main auditorium. So left almost alone on Ferguson Avenue is the Baptist church, its latest minister R.M. Carkner says. Yet the Salvation Army Barracks is still at the Amwell Street corner across from the Attorney Hotel and, although unused, the Roman Catholic chapel still stands beside Marcella Street as does the Methodist rectory and its former church building beside Blackwall Street. In April, bricklayers resume work on Haileybury's new Presbyterian Church; winter had come last December before the roof was on. Now, though, shingles cover the gable slopes. With its interior designed to seat 350 people with extra space to build a gallery for another 100, the Presbyterian Church is set far enough back from Browning Street to allow for a north wing and pews for 300 more.

Haileybury's new Methodist church, northeast corner of Rorke and Main, 1912

One half mile south along Georgina Avenue, Clem Foster has donated eleven acres between Elliott and Little streets where the Roman Catholic Sisters of Providence are building a $30,000 hospital of Lake Temiskaming limestone. Clem Foster had bought the land from Marcella Lawlor, now remarried to E.C. Kingswell, who has no interest in keeping her first husband's old farm intact.

The Roman Catholics are also adding a two room annex to their two-storey, four room separate school building on Rorke Avenue diagonally across Cecil Street corner from the public school. Mrs. Colbourn, the principal, emphasizes how chalk-dust-choking teachers Mrs. D.J. Charlebois, Miss Noonan, Miss Pelletier and two sisters of the Assumption are anxious for freedom from cramped classrooms. Joe Brisebois, chairman of the Separate School Board, George T. Smith, secretary-treasurer, and the rest of the members Dr. Codd, Ben Killoran, L. Gagnon and A. Grenon promise the healthier space will be ready next September.

Haileyburians at N.C.R. Vendome Hotel stop
Left to right: J. Bray,_____, _____, S.M. Henrotin, Leo Erenhous,
Percy Dunbar, _____, Don Jacobi

Thanks to the efforts of George T. Smith who is also on the High School Board and those of Bob Shillington, M.P.P., and Frank Cochrane, the Ontario government has just granted $5,000 to establish the new high school's department of minerology. An excited Charlie Spearman already has plans for a laboratory in the school's basement. Having arrived from Kenora as the school's principal in charge of completing its classroom layout during the closing months and winter of 1910, Principal W.A. Wilson remembers how the first class started in the old public school building on Ferguson Avenue with eighteen students. Last September with the high school opened on Latchford Street, enrollment swelled to 103. And now with more students travelling by Nipissing Central trolley from Cobalt, the school's assembly hall on the second floor is short of chairs. That the attractive school might even someday soon run out of standing room became a possibility on March 12 when Nipissing Central's manager Uttley set a "Special Scholar's Rate" for high school students from Cobalt and North Cobalt: ten tickets for twenty-five cents.

N.C.R. trolley turns at Blackwell Street and Ferguson Avenue corner, Haileybury

Principal Wilson teaches mathematics and science, W.C. Clarke teaches English and Latin while Miss Arletta Nelson, has moderns, art and commercial subjects. Who will replace Misses McGregor and Nellie Arthur next year? No one knows. But chairman Smith and fellow board members Fred Preston, secretary-treasurer J. McNairn-Hall, John Shibley, J.L. McDougall, G.T. Hamilton, H.T. Routly, J.E. McCuaig, J.T. McMahon assure all parents they have several teacher applications on file from last year.

Six months it has taken, though, for Haileybury's Anglican church to find a replacement for Rev. Harper. As Deacon, Paul Cobbold has read part of the Sunday services while the ministers from New Liskeard and Cobalt have taken turns giving communion. Finally in April, Rev. J.C. Popey appeared. And now, in May, he feels especially welcome when Frank Atkinson takes him for a buggy ride out the West Road to view his Firstbrook township farm, the broken part of lot two, concession three. Returning three years ago from their farming sojourn on Vancouver Island, Frank, his brothers James and Stephen use these eighty-two acres on the east shore of Moose Lake as their latest home. Unlike their youngest, married brother Siegfried, they have remained devoted bachelors roving Canada for some sense of permanence.

Better to roost awhile in Haileybury, they have now decided and confine their roaming to Northern Ontario for some chance at mineral treasure. Certainly chances are flourishing. Why just a week ago, McIntyre Porcupine delivered its first five gold bars to Alfred Young, George Bagshaw and Charles Richardson as payment towards money owed them for selling their property share. Seriously short of cash McIntyre Mine could have used this $12,927.90 worth of gold, yet it cannot risk foreclosure. Meanwhile free of debt on their nearby property, Noah Timmins and syndicate partners from LaRose Mine days are counting on the new Hollinger mill starting to repay their investment in June.

Not only has Porcupine dug into rich ore, but Kirkland Lake is showing strong hints of doing the same. When Harry Oakes and the Tough brothers started February 20 assessment work on their north claim beside Cliff Burnside's trench, they exposed in the first hour of digging north a quartz vein in a belt of porphyry. Within a week they found an ore shoot assaying between $200 to $400 a ton over a four foot width. This mineral showing, though, some fifteen to twenty feet long, has since disappeared under a deep swamp to the west. Almost at the same time as this first discovery, they trenched another rock showing and panned $600 ore before quicksand began filling the hole as Harry Oakes says, "Near the Lebel township line at the corner of a Burnside claim,...a short crack there panned very heavily in gold." But the most important vein they found shortly after May's snow melted; about 120 feet long, its crack shows rich highgrade. And as soon as handpicked samples processed through the Northern Customs mill at Cobalt gave spectacular $150 to $1,200 values, Harry and the Tough brothers began blasting out an open cut. And more crosstrenching in the opposite east direction of the other quicksand threatened vein has revealed assays of $200 to $300 per ton across an eighteen inch to three foot width.

Excited by these discoveries, Weldon Young, who has bought Ed Hargreaves' share in the Kirkland Lake claims for $7,500 is presently in Buffalo, New York, trying to raise enough money to put down two short diamond drill holes on the neighbouring Wright-Hargreaves land. Unlike his brother-in-law partner who has a remnant of family inheritance to support himself, Ed needed the windfall sales profit to comfort his family's life in Haileybury. Not Swift Burnside, though; like the Tough brothers and Harry Oakes, he has been trenching his own ground since February; but as yet, without similar results.

Having more experienced reasons to expect highgrade results from its proven silver property at Cobalt, Nipissing Mines has started pumping jet streams of water against the eastern hillside sloping up from Cobalt Lake. Larger this is than any magician's stage act, shoppers along Lang Street say as they gawk at ground disappearing across the lake. Gushing streams chew away the top soil, bare the bedrock; trees, stones and boulders tumble down into the lake. By summer's end most of Nipissing Hill will stand naked gray.

So far no hiding places of important veins have been successfully exposed, but with so much silver found close by, every underground and surface foot of this area is worth prospecting.

Haileybury Road (Lang Street), Cobalt east side up from the Square - OA-14998-13

Haileybury Road (Lang Street), Cobalt looking south toward T.&N.O. station - OA-S-15826

Yet of what help are any more silver discoveries to Cobalt's municipal finances? Not much. But a Monday, March 25 meeting at the town hall did try to solve the nagging contradiction. Board of Trade president Ralph Taylor said the provincial government should give all local mining taxes collected to Cobalt, not just half. Mayor R.Z. Trudell agreed. So poor is Cobalt, councillor Taylor Pipe explained, the town is destroying itself: forced to impose a property tax rate of thirty-five to thirty-nine mills, almost four percent on valuations far higher than the properties are worth, the town is driving present residents and businesses to move elsewhere. Arthur Ferland, though, as reeve of Coleman township argued against sending a delegation to Queens Park. And Judge Mahon added that the province's half share of mining tax money was meant for all the people of Ontario. Then Buffalo Mine manager T.R. Jones suggested Coleman township, besides spending $10,000 this year on Cobalt streets, should help pay for the debentures Cobalt had issued to build its water and sewage system. And Reeve Ferland promised his township would start paying half the $75,000 debenture cost. This township had originally guaranteed a share; now was the time to honour it. But what of Cobalt's other major expense? No one had any suggestion of how to lower the town's insurance rates excessively high ever since 1909's fire so easily consumed the many wooden buildings along Lang Street.

Cobalt, however, will have its own fruit and vegetable market this summer beside J.B. Moyneur's store at the foot of Argentite Street, near where the streetcar stops. And north of there will be the town's new garbage incinerator. Two weeks ago, at a March 9 meeting, town council, faced with the end of its six year lease on the Clear Lake site and the threatened seepage of garbage wastes into the town's nearby Mud Lake water supply, decided to move the dump to the low swamp area closer to town. By July, a town bylaw should succeed in prohibiting all dumping at Clear Lake.

Thanks to "young real estate agent" Talbot Dunbar of Haileybury the May 18 evening stage performance at Cobalt's Lyric Theatre proves successful. Earlier at five o'clock this Saturday afternoon the play's two stars Jeanne Tower, billed as the "American Beauty", and Vernon Wallace decided to rent a canoe at Haileybury dock for a relaxing paddle. At warnings the whitecaps out in the middle of the lake meant trouble, they laughed. Just look at the giant patches of sunlight caressing those same waves, they said; the grey clouds will fully part and the sun will lull the waters, they called back as their canoe slipped out into the dock's calm south side shelter. Yet once around by the dock's exposed east side, their canoe began to pitch. And seventy-five yards north of the dock when Vernon Wallace tried to turn back, it capsized. Seeing the spill from the front porch of the Matabanick Hotel, Talbot Dunbar ran out to the end of the dock, stripped off his coat and shoes, jumped into the lake and swam to the rescue. Clinging to the wave-tossed canoe for fifteen minutes the two wide-eyed actors were unable to say a word, but Talbot had them grab his hands from the other side of the overturned boat. At least he could support their weight until someone else came. David Jarvis and Tom Montgomery had also seen the accident. And as four foot waves washed the canoe and its survivors closer they pushed out planks from the end of the dock to help them stay afloat. Playing their parts this night in *The White Sister*, Jeanne Tower and Vernon Wallace look out beyond the footlights for Talbot's reassuring face. They guess he is still drying himself off at his Brewster Street home in Haileybury but they have invited him for dinner tomorrow at the Matabanick Hotel. While someone else goes for a canoe ride.

Matabanick Hotel front porch, original Haileybury Public School in background

Not even a lakeful of water could have drowned last week's fire at his Energite Explosive Company's plant, a half mile out the West Road from Haileybury, manager C.C. Kippen sighs. Once the fire, which started in a crusher at two in the afternoon spread to the chlorite-mix, flames immediately leaped to the ceiling of the 100 foot long, 30 foot wide building. The 350 pounds of cheddite powder merely burned but a tub of paraffin exploded a 40 foot column of flame skywards. Firemen assisted by the men of the factory did try to tear holes through the building's tin sheathing and spray water inside; but with asbestos sheets placed between the wooden studs and another layer of tin covering the inside wall, they could only stand safely back as the inpenetrable factory and all its machinery crumpled. At least no one was injured. The women had fled towards town. And soon, within two more days, everyone should be back to work in a temporary building.

Haileybury's police chief Paddy Collins and constable Jack Fleming spent a talkative afternoon warning people scrambling up Browning Street for a look at the fire not to cross the tracks in case of another explosion. Yet the policemen never dreamed last night's high wind would knock down the tall wireless pole Thomas Edison had left abandoned southwest of the railway station, up the slight rise from the town's water reservoir on Whitney Street. Fortunately no one was ambling underneath.

Haileybury's fire engine, hose wagon practising beside Preston's Store at Main Street, Ferguson Avenue intersection

With construction now started on extending the N.C.R. trolley tracks to New Liskeard, fewer people will have to amble on foot or ride a rough horse from one town to the other. And the four mile extension will not take too long to lay. After placing new tracks from Haileybury's Vendome Hotel to join the spur-line at the foot of Florence Street workmen will then move one and a half miles north to lay more new track from the spur line for a few hundred feet before crossing a small bridge built over Dickson's Creek to the T.&N.O.'s main line, from where in front of Professor Sharp's house on the outskirts of town new tracks will slope down on to LakeShore Road and the final Wabis River stop.

Already New Liskeard is digging up the last of LakeShore Road for water and sewer pipelines before the workmen arrive to grade and lay the rails over top. Cobalt wishes it was not left with the summer's expense of smoothing out Cobalt Street hill's pitted mess of water and sewage pipeline mud. Its own pipeline streets long levelled, Haileybury can now afford to grade and roll the final stretch of Meridian Avenue smooth from Marcella to Main Street. And set a concrete walkway along the west side.

That additional Nipissing Central tracks will bring the three towns closer together is worth the price of $55,901.56. Yet, on June 8, no price, it seems, may ever bring the towns together—especially Haileybury and New Liskeard. For this day a special edition of the *Haileyburian* headlines an "Announcement by the Cabinet of the legislature of Ontario that Temiskaming has been formed into a judicial district and that Haileybury is the judicial centre of that district.'' Tom Jarrett, the newspaper's managing editor, also chairman of the town's Finance Committee, has collaborated with Herb Day on this ''District Seat Edition''. Formerly in charge of the *Haileyburian,* presently the town's assessor, tax collector and market inspector, Herb Day has briefly returned to newspaper work as Haileybury's publicity commissioner.

Herbert Day in front garden of his Russel Street home, Roman Catholic cathedral in background, Haileybury

Jarrett and Day boast that the Ontario Cabinet has made ''no haphazard judgement..., but that their decision has been made after long and careful investigation of the situation, for the choice of the government has been praised by every unbiased observer who has ventured an opinion.''

''Haileybury,'' they say, ''has the finest waterworks system in Temiskaming,'' and ''a most efficient incinerator for garbage.'' As a lumbering centre ''upwards of $350,000 is distributed from the Haileybury offices of some of the largest lumbering concerns in Ontario.'' Furthermore, ''as the Haileybury spur, now under construction, connects directly with the waterfront...it is only reasonable to expect that as Mr. Foster has laboured night and day to get the spur built, and has said that he would have the mill running when the spur was built, it will not be long before the Haileybury sawmill will be running and turning out its full capacity of lumber.'' What of other industries? The Haileybury Brick Company ''is having its brick plant at the south end of town entirely remodelled and rebuilt.'' The Energite Explosive Company intends to rebuild a fireproof factory ''with a much larger capacity'' than the one recently burned. Mention also J.W. Noble's Nipissing Laundry on upper Browning Street, beside John Shibley's house; it employs twenty-five people. Mention Dunbar's Planing Mill, beside the tracks south of the station. Mention the town's athletic grounds, its race track. Mention J. McGillicuddy's Haileybury Band and its ''fine orchestra, which has been kept in practice during the past spring at the Star Theatre.''

And now the Ontario government will build a large courthouse in Haileybury to serve all Temiskaming. Not a corresponding jail, though. Any criminals with long sentences will continue doing their time at North Bay or penitentiaries farther south.

The *Haileyburian's* District Seat Edition further says "that Haileybury is the one spot in the whole of the North Country suited for a transportation centre." Beside the T.&N.O. and Nipissing Central railways, beside Temiskaming Navigation boats and wagon roads, central Haileybury reaches Cochrane, Cobalt, New Liskeard, White River, Guiges, Ville Marie, Silver Centre, North and South Temiskaming. From Haileybury's 800 foot long wharf with large store houses, offices and waiting room at its broad head, Temiskaming Navigation Company steamers, in 1911, shipped 3,687.17 tons of freight:

To	Ville Marie	415.57
	Guiges	125.55
	Silver Centre	470.74
	North Temiskaming	99.00
	New Liskeard	39.07
	Temiskaming	82.34
	Fabre	20.74
	Flag Stations	174.06

The gross tonnage of outgoing freight from Haileybury by rail, in 1911, was 18,626; the gross incoming freight was 17,361.

Holy Cross Cathedral, Convent, and Dr. Codd's house, Haileybury

The *Haileyburian* editors describe their town as the "educational centre of North Ontario." Why does it occupy "a pre-eminent position in this respect as in fact practically all other respects?" Haileybury, they say, "is willing to expend over one-third or thirty-seven and one half percent of its total taxes on education. Although excessive enrollment at the new public school has forced Principal McFarlane to shift junior pupils into two rooms of the old Ferguson Avenue school, the town's public library on the lower floor does not face eviction; if the large enrolment persists, the School Board promises to build more classroom space on to the newest Rorke Avenue building.

Cobalt is still too shocked by a June 5 fire to congratulate Haileybury. Last Wednesday evening Alfred Scott, stage manager of Cobalt's Lyric Theatre, spied smoke rising from between dressing room floorboards. Rushing outside he ran to box number 23 opposite the Prospect Hotel and rang the alarm at 9:05 o'clock. Meanwhile the theatre audience also noticing smoke from the side wing of the stage during Ramsay and Weiss' vaudeville act had already begun leaving. To calm everyone Harry Brown continued playing his piano. By the short minute Alfred Scott returned to the front door of the Opera House choking smoke blocked his way inside. Just then Harry Brown staggered out after the last of the theatre-goers. As part of this night's audience Cobalt fireman Tom O'Gorman had gone backstage at the first hint of smoke to realize the danger and help people leave. Within five minutes of Scott's alarm, flames from the theatre's stage location in the southeast corner of the building could be seen flaring along the front roof edge of the Opera House with all its windows and porticoed door facing the Square spouting fire, Once engineer Billy McFarland's steam engine began pumping lakeshore water, fire chief Kappele's men were spraying two streams on the front. A third hose was at the eastern railway station side where flames were bursting through the ground floor windows.

By 9:15 o'clock the building's whole wooden interior was a roaring inferno. And, flames had licked along the front from the Lyric Theatre door past Coyne's shop to Black's store and Carr's larger one at the Presley Street corner.

Quickly alarmed Haileybury and New Liskeard firemen came to help halt the blaze from spreading through the business heart of town. Because the furnace heat had splintered Kellock's main floor windows in the Hunter Block across the Square, Cobalt's firemen had already turned their hoses in that direction. What about the Cobalt Hotel on the Opera House's other side? With only eight feet of space between them, the two buildings must surely flame together.

What about the buildings along Prospect Avenue and Silver Street? After Haileybury fire chief Ike Quinn's brigade of engineer Tom Lemon, Tommy Currie, Billy Beattie, George Reilly, Irwin Berry, Jack McNish, Phil Jacobs, Merle Davis and John Campbell arrived in a special N.C.R. trolley from the North Cobalt carbarn with their hose wagon racing behind, the men connected to the hydrant next to the Mines Hospital on Silver Street. Just in time to build a western wall of water. For, after half an hour, sparks were eating into the roof of Galoska's nearby Presley Street block of stores. The water doused them but then the Cobalt Hotel ignited. And more sparks flew on to Harrington's restaurant and back to Galoska's.

To keep the steam engine pumping hose water Constables Sam Newton and Fred Williams pressed a horse and rig from the Square to haul coal from a car on the T.&N.O. siding. Assistants on the steam engine, Jim Cornell and Bob Fairbrother, shovelled like madmen.

Since the telegraph-telephone pole in front of the Opera House had burned and threatened to fall, its swaying wires were cut to protect the fire fighters below. By then, though, the New Liskeard brigade was travelling to Cobalt. Station agent Goodman had put together a special train; but "Reddie" Fraught, the New Liskeard operator, along with three assistants had to go in advance of the engine in a slow handcar flagging down any T.&N.O. train which had no telegraph warning of their unscheduled trip over the main line. By the 1:30 time New Liskeard fire chief John Lever arrived with Ace Jewell, Jack McLean, Angus McLean, Oscar Cox, Howard Williams, John Armstrong, Fred Thompson, Bill Taylor and others, the fire was well under control. At 3:00 o'clock all the Tri-Town firemen surrounded a smouldering mass of flickering ashes.

Cobalt fire, Opera House and hotel, June 5, 1912

Although closest to the flames, the scorched Bank of Commerce, with the Nipissing Stores Block and the Town Hall survived. But a wood ash wasteland lies within the area bounded by Prospect Avenue, Silver Street, Grandview Avenue and Commission Street. Gone is the Opera House Block and its Lyric Theatre, Leonard Coyne's Gents' furnishing store and A.H. Black's jewellery shop. Gone are its offices for Coleman township, for the Customs, for doctors Schmidt and Clark, for town solicitor George Ross, for Len Foster's Nipissing Land Company, for A.L. Herbert's custom brokers.

Gone is the Cobalt Hotel with Art Abbott's barber shop. Gone is Milton Carr & Sons department store. Gone is Charles Reckin's flour and feed building. Gone is the Hunter and Moore building, McLaughlin's tailor shop, the Mine's Chemical Supply Company, the Galoska building and Mrs. Harrington's restaurant. Especially bitter is Elizabeth Harrington's loss. First coming north to operate Nipissing Mine's earliest cook camp she had succeeded in building a restaurant in South Porcupine. It burned in last year's fire. Now this.

Cobalt fire ruins, June 6, 1912

Cobalt fire ruins, June 6, 1912

Most of the burned buildings were made of wood sheeted in tin. Along with P.J. Finlan, Herb Wallace, in syndicate partnership with his brother Jack and father Tom's Cobalt Standard Mining Exchange business, had built the Opera House. Never believing its lavish wooden frame would end like this. Most recently Herb and P.J. Hart controlled the Lyric theatres. Today P.J. Hart is still without personal belongings; and as Coleman township clerk he may have a temporary office in the Royal Exchange building, but an office empty of records, all lost in the fire. But no one died.

Boats docked at Haileybury, C.C. Farr steers his 'Jennie M.'

More numbed by Haileybury's District Seat victory, the *New Liskeard Speaker* snarls

To those on the ground floor it seems rather strange that a town that cannot decently support one newspaper should be given preference over several other towns whose citizens are a hundred percent more enterprising along pure business lines.

Suddenly, however New Liskeard has no time to think of Haileybury. On June 17, Daniel T.K. (Mac) McEwen one of the town's most enterprising lawyers dies. Despite his crutches, in the shape of three-legged tripods whose long handles he so often pulled together for a chair, no one ever thought of his heart finally failing. Then next Sunday morning Tom McCamus' sister

Lucy dies. Nine years ago both men helped organize and shape New Ontario's first mining company. For fifteen years Lucy has lived in New Liskeard, always in praise of her brother. As honour guard, New Liskeard police chief Paddy Miller accompanies both funeral processions west on Whitewood Avenue. Having left the similar position in Haileybury to succeed ailing chief C.E. Symons and his temporary replacement Mr. Wadsworth, Paddy not only patrols the sidewalks but has a farm of several acres at the north end of May Street. D.T.K. McEwen was his lawyer.

Maple Leaf Hotel, Haileybury

New Liskeard's Dr. John Duncan McNaughton feels little kindness towards the newly chosen District Town. One recent Saturday afternoon he went to Haileybury to race his horse Togo. C.C. Farr, though, as track judge disqualified the horse. So disgusted was the doctor he vows never to race again and instead will hitch Togo in turns with the little bronco Mae to pull his buggy on medical visits into the townships.

Yet life ticks on. New Liskeard's George Taylor Hardware buys the surviving stock of Mines Chemical Supply Company and opens a Mines Assay supply department in the Cobalt store. Always expanding his sons' business, George Taylor opened the most distant store at Larder City. Now five years later he plans a farther one next year at Matheson and if the North Country continues to prosper, the year after at Cochrane.

Maybe this New Liskeard company is following M.J. O'Brien's example of self reliance. O'Brien who helped finance the new Wabi Iron Works to guarantee his mine's supply of stamp mill parts is presently strengthening his Cobalt Foundry. In every possible way. On superintendent

J.J. Evans' advice, he has just lured E.M. Houghton, a trained pattern maker, away from Nipissing Mines' machine shop. Only arriving at Cobalt six months ago to join his sister Polly and her husband Tom Pinder, Eddy jumps at the chance to work in a foundry again. Even though he will sacrifice any excuse to ride George Brewer's brand new Albion Char-A-Banc bus which now runs a regular route over the Ferland Avenue railway bridge, past his new Cobalt Foundry workplace towards the Coleman township mine he just quit.

But how long will Eddy's new job last? Since the massive Opera House-Cobalt Hotel blaze so many more fires have threatened the town not even the Cobalt Foundry seems safe. On June 18 an oil stove on the first floor of the Imperial Bank caught fire and filled the building with smoke. On June 25 a bucket of coal tar being heated on the roof of the Hunter Block caught fire. Without William Kennedy and his friends forming a bucket brigade before a fire hose could be stretched to the wooden roof, the high wind could have easily blown flames out of control. That same Tuesday afternoon City of Cobalt miners were trenching surface bedrock on the ash strewn site of Carr's former store. Beter there than shovelling away two nearby feet of overburden sand where the Lyric Theatre building once stood. Searching for mineral vien exposures above a drift crossing under Silver Street to a point 200 feet below Galoska's Store site, the mining company has little time for mourning. On June 29 a night-time Argentite Street fire, started in the Chinese laundry between the Crown Hotel and Argentite House, not only burns flat the laundry and adjacent buildings but also the Leland House.

Cobalt Foundry at viewer's left. Campbell and Deyell Plant to right

Although this summer's heavy rain, which seems to fall everywhere except on Cobalt's fires, could easily mire Brewer's two cylinder bus in roadway puddles of churned mud, tourists in Temagami heartily applaud the well watered abundance of flowers at the railway station there. What colours!

Manager of the Temagami Steamboat and Hotel Company, George Irwin, who convinced the T.&N.O. Commission to plant the large flower bed shaped after the village name, can now point to increasing numbers of holidaying passengers attracted north. Despite this summer's wetness. After sleeping at the Ronnoco Hotel with its dining room and dance floor, for $3.00 a night, up to three hundred shirtsleeved people can board the steamer *Belle of Temagami* on a round trip to Bear Island for $1.50. Fifteen miles down the northeast arm, Temagami Inn can accommodate a hundred guests. Seventeen miles farther to the northwest corner of the lake on Deer Island near Sharp Rock Inlet is the two hundred guest Lady Evelyn Hotel. Alongside this two-storey pile of ornate logs, a store and post office wean most homesick guests away from daydreams of metal clanking city streets. And if canoeists or fishermen need more shopping, Hudson's Bay Company factor Harry Woods' outfitter's store is only a few dips of the paddle away on Bear Island.

Temagami T.&N.O. Station garden

Staring at Temagami station, twenty-six year old William Joy, who came to Canada six months ago and is now on his way to work as master nurseryman for Colonel Hay in Haileybury, rubs his amazed eyes at the lusty growth of so many flowers. Less reason do he and wife Grace have to worry the Hays might be deceiving him about the beauty of Temiskaming gardens.

And when he does stand in the middle of the Hays' garden laid out between Amwell and Marcella streets, he realizes why people today still label Haileybury as Little England after C.C. Farr's original colonization dream: for Hay's expanse of lawns, shrubs, flowers and orchard trees is like being inside a green cabbage. Yet who broke the big branch in the apple tree?

Children last fall, Trott the Hays' tall, lantern-jawed butler says. Immaculate in his white and red striped, brass-buttoned waistcoat under a white jacket, he angrily recalls them bounding to school, spying the red fruit, sneaking back after dark and filling their pockets.

Having moved from a first rented house on Latchford Street to buy his present one on Marcella, Principal McFarlane lives close enough by to understand the temptation of the Hays' fruit trees. And the need to restrain his own sons. The two white haired teachers who loyally followed him from Carleton Place have warned their pupils about trespassing. Miss Eva Findlay, though, teaches younger, less daring ones; not Miss Sarah Flegg, however, who shakes her "frizzy" head of hair. A black apron with pockets for chalk, blackboard brush and pencils protects her dress as she patrols classroom rows of grade seven desks. And hanging by a leather thong from her right wrist a layered canvas-rubber strap warns all lawbreakers of teeth-clenching punishment.

Even school board Chairman John Rankin pales at second-hand versions of her hell-fire warnings. Other board members Herb Day, Paul Cobbold, Rev. J.A. Donnell, W.E. Buchan and W.H. McLaughlin prefer not to hear. Principal McFarlane keeps to his grade eight classroom. Unable to match Sarah's warrior stature, Misses M.A. Smillie, G. Wills, E. Menzies, Violette Archibald, Hazel Evans, H.J. Stewart and Margaret McDonald worry whether their teaching smiles are a sign of weakness.

Soon these unmarried teachers, many of whom live in Stitt's Temperance House on Broadway Street, may feel less conspicuous with board and lodgings in New Liskeard. For on October 4, the *New Liskeard Speaker* reports Nipissing Central trolley cars should be reaching temporary end of steel at LakeShore Road and Whitewood Avenue by Monday, October 21. Because the track crew needs special curved steel for the right angled turns on and off Whitewood Avenue, it cannot yet complete the line to the terminus on Armstrong Street at Wabis River bridge. But when it does, this final point will remain the northern end of the line "until such time as it is decided to pass on to the White River settlement."

To harden the clay bed under its extension north, Nipissing Central Railway has graded and coated Haileybury and New Liskeard streets with sixteen cars of gravel from Cassidy pit. Yet Paddy Fleming who quit managing underground miners to buy Haileybury's Vendome Hotel complains not enough fill was dumped into greasy ruts left beside his hotel, where last year's extra terminal siding track was located. Within the projected cost of $31.83 for the total job in the two towns the T.&N.O. Commission through its Nipissing Central foster child, promises to do what it can.

Stitt House, Broadway Street, Haileybury

For the September 18 reception of former Prime Minister Sir Wilfred Laurier, the Nipissing Central line between Cobalt and Haileybury is gravel smooth. This day to unveil an oil portrait in memory of Dr. William Henry Drummond at the opening of the Y.M.C.A. building on Silver Street, Canada's statesman comes to Cobalt. After the reading room ceremony he tours the library, billiards room and gymnasium, then downstairs sees the swimming pool and three-lane bowling alley. Before a standing-room-only crowd at the arena he praises Cobalt's progress from its Young Men's Christian Reading Room beginning at the town Square till now when Cobalt boasts the first Y.M.C.A. building north of Toronto. Later in the afternoon Clem Foster as secretary of Temiskaming's Liberal Association entertains at his Haileybury home before they take an evening trip on the *Meteor* across the lake to another meeting in Ville Marie.

New Presbyterian church, Haileybury

Haileybury view from Lake Temiskaming - OA-15380-117

Stations— Elk Lake Branch

Earlton........................	Mileage	0
McCool......................	"	5
Kenabeck....................	"	10 3/4
Osseo Siding..............	"	14 3/4
Mountain Chutes........	"	17 3/4
Wabun........................	"	22
Beacon........................	"	25
Elk Lake.....................	"	28 1/2

Steady summer rain has not only made a mud bath of Haileybury and New Liskeard streets but combined with a shortage of workers and steel beams for the Montreal River bridge, it has delayed construction of the branch rail line to Elk Lake. Just to build the 750 foot long timber trestle sixty-five feet above the swollen Baptiste River has taken four months, and it is still unfinished. Do not expect the first train to arrive at Elk Lake until January, at the earliest, the T.&N.O. Commission warns. And people along the twenty-eight mile line will have to wait until next spring for station freight sheds and section houses. Tight lipped—since Earlton was chosen the departure point for Elk Lake—Charlton, can, at least, thank the Commission for extending its Long Lake siding another 1,255 feet to the Government wharf. Yet Latchford feels deserted. Over the past five years its Bay Lake location has served as the main rail depot and harbour for summer ships steaming up Montreal River to Elk Lake and Gowganda. Now the Earlton branch line will quickly render these ships obsolete. A grim irony, since the new Bay Lake dam has already started raising Montreal River water to drown out the worst part of Pork Rapids portage and make steamer travel faster. Regardless, the port of Latchford is about to die.

Surely with weatherproof, year-round transport into Elk Lake, many of the Montreal River-Gowganda area mines should start to explore their ground again. Follow our lead, the Mann mineowners say. But few of Gowganda's other rich surface discoveries have continued to depth, except for M.J. O'Brien's Miller Lake Mine which has had little trouble finding enough highgrade silver to load annual sleighs over the winter road to Charlton.

Yet Seneca-Superior Silver Mine's surprise October 11 discovery, at Cobalt, of 3,000 ounce to the ton highgrade silver while reworking the abandoned Kerry Mining Company lease under Cart Lake trumpets the value of a second look at any of Temiskaming's older properties. Named after Seneca's president, Harry Worth, the vein, mine manager Bob Lyman confides, will pay big dividends.

Admittedly, though, more of Cobalt's mining men are starting to think gold. How much longer can any of them afford deeper underground mining costs for sixty cents an ounce silver ore? Especially when the same cost at Porcupine is producing twenty dollars an ounce gold. Although too close to the flash-in-the-pan vicinity of Larder Lake, the rock structure of Kirkland Lake may be worth investigating. But the mines at nearby Swastika are barely meeting their payrolls. And even the Porcupine mines have not yet dug up final proof their surface wealth runs deep.

Cobalt T.&N.O. station, former Cobalt Hotel at viewer's left, beside former Opera House, 1911

Despite this year's rain and mining skepticism, a few men have been handsteeling and blasting rock at Kirkland Lake. And before anyone else could take a step, Harry Oakes, on July 30, staked two water claims on the lake's south bay, hugging what he thinks is the western extension of Bill Wright's vein discovery. On August 26, however, Wright woke first to leapfrog over Harry and stake the last lake claim, next to Reamsbottom's west shore property. Then with money from his brother Louis and sister Gertrude, Harry Oakes on September 16 finally registered the agreed-upon transfer of McDougall's claim from last summer. And a week later he registered a second transfer of Minaker's claim neighbouring west along the lakeshore. Now on his original McDougall transfer claim he and Ernie Martin are handsteeling a two-compartment shaft. From their low slung canvas tent in front of which rock chunks circle a mound of ashes heating the blackened bottom of their rabbit stew pot, the two men lurch down a narrow path towards their deepening shaft. The fall wind has blown yellow leaves out on to the lake's rippling waters but when the morning sun shines surrounding birch tree bones white, it is time to drill.

Ernie holds the steel. Last night, after their small forge had fired red hot the steel's chisel end, Harry hammered it sharp, cooled it in water, rubbed it sand clean then waited for the right straw-coloured temper. Quickly Ernie now turns the steel in the angled hole as Harry's seven pound hammer hits thirty-five strokes a minute. Adding water to the deepening hole and wrapping a sock around the steel at ground level, Ernie soon shouts "Mud." Unable to turn the steel because of rock cuttings at the bottom, he must clean out the drill hole with a stick. Maybe it is time to change to a longer steel. Down the hole it goes, wrap the sock against the hammer's water splashing blows, strike, turn and water. Taking two hours to complete a four foot hole how many can they drill today for the next blast? Down they go. And Harry thanks his brother and sister for making this single-jacking way possible.

Some ore from open pits along the vein assays thirty dollars a ton and the shaft is exposing small patches of gold. Once deep enough, Harry plans to drive a crosscut tunnel north under the lake to intersect Wright's vein. And his sister who listened to Harry's hopes as they walked the rocky lake edge this summer has pledged more of her savings.

Does a woman look out of place wandering these lost bush trails? Not if you know eighteen year old Mabel Fetterly who lives in Swastika. And what about Roza Brown who also prospects, in between batches of laundry. Prying outcrops apart, their pickaxes ring just as bellnote clear as any man's.

Today, though, Bill Wright's pickaxe rests in troubled silence. Noticing in the mining recorder's office at Haileybury that Wright overstaked his last forty acre claim in August, Fred Connell hurriedly organized his brother, Harold, Arthur Cockeram and Shirley Cragg to restake the excess seven and a half acres. And they are willing to bet their fractional claim stands up in court.

Ed Hargreaves blesses himself for selling his share of what could become for Bill Wright a Kirkland Lake headache. With his sale earnings Ed has bought a piano for wife Frances, and torn out the inside of their Lawlor Street home so he and carpenter Tom Poppleton could redesign, paint and wallpaper. And now Ed, once trained as an artist, thinks of starting his own business decorating other Haileybury buildings.

Maybe, however, Kirkland Lake ground is worth fighting over. All summer, Mine Captain John Murphy has supervised bagging handpicked highgrade from the open cut on the Tough-Oakes' number two vein. Walter Little has contracted with George and Tom Tough, who have some spare cash to spend, that as soon as December ice coats Kirkland Lake he will sled out the estimated two tons of ore to Swastika station. And with his five mile trail packed snow hard through the bush he can start hauling regular supplies and mining equipment to the minesite.

Dynamite might be in short supply, though. For on Wednesday, October 25, at 11:30 a.m., the Energite Explosive Company's factory at Haileybury blows up. Almost five months ago, fire destroyed the original building. But there was no harmful explosion. Yet this morning with work on the new building almost completed and factory workers manufacturing Cheddite in the temporary one nearby, powder materials catch fire in the mixer. Immediately manager H. Long tells the workers to flee then shouts, "Turn on the hose." Within a minute a deafening explosion shatters the site; a huge inverted cone of reddish, orange flame surmounted by swirling black clouds of smoke shoots skywards. Houses jump. Window glass shatters throughout Haileybury. Fortunately, school window sills are higher than the heads of children sitting under the gust of slicing slivers. Clutching the water hose, Long dies. So does Robert Young who was installing the heating system. So do carpenters Tom Poppleton and John McLaughlin. As well Fred Erickson and a married woman who went back for her dinner pail and cloak. Even those who escaped are thrown off their feet. Yet two hundred yards up the West Road the dynamite magazine remains intact. Not Tom Poppleton's family, though. His widow is left with young sons Jack, Jim and Russell.

Once Robert Campbell saw panic-stricken workers fleeing for the road he started running for the protection of his stone house. But before he could reach the door a part of the factory's smoke stack hurtled across the road, striking him in the back. As he sprawled on the ground other exploded bits flew upwards with the mushroom cloud. Made from limestone blocks he had handsteeled out of its six foot deep cellar, Campbell's house stood firm, not even a window cracked. Three years ago he had fortunately moved his family here from a makeshift house across the road, close by the explosives plant. First moving to Haileybury in 1898, he married six years later Ann Johnson whose parents Charles and Letitia had originally bought his present land between C.C. Farr's acreage and John Westron's farm. Their purchase had saved their daughter, her husband and grandchildren's lives.

East of the explosion, debris litters Clem Foster's farm where Ambrose Dupuis pastures his dairy herd. But not a scratch scars any cow. Perhaps the incessant rainstorms which have driven the animals into the habit of sheltering themselves on the other side of the barn saved them.

Energite Explosive's Company staff at Haileybury plant

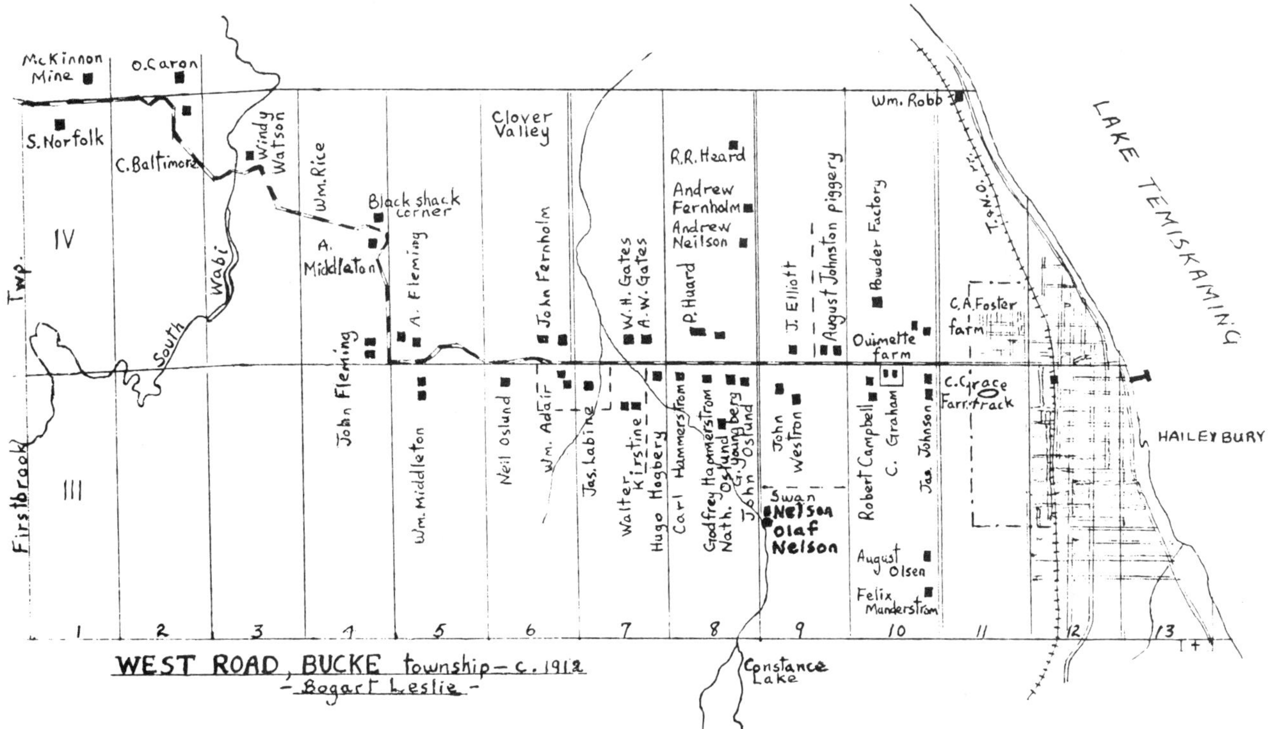

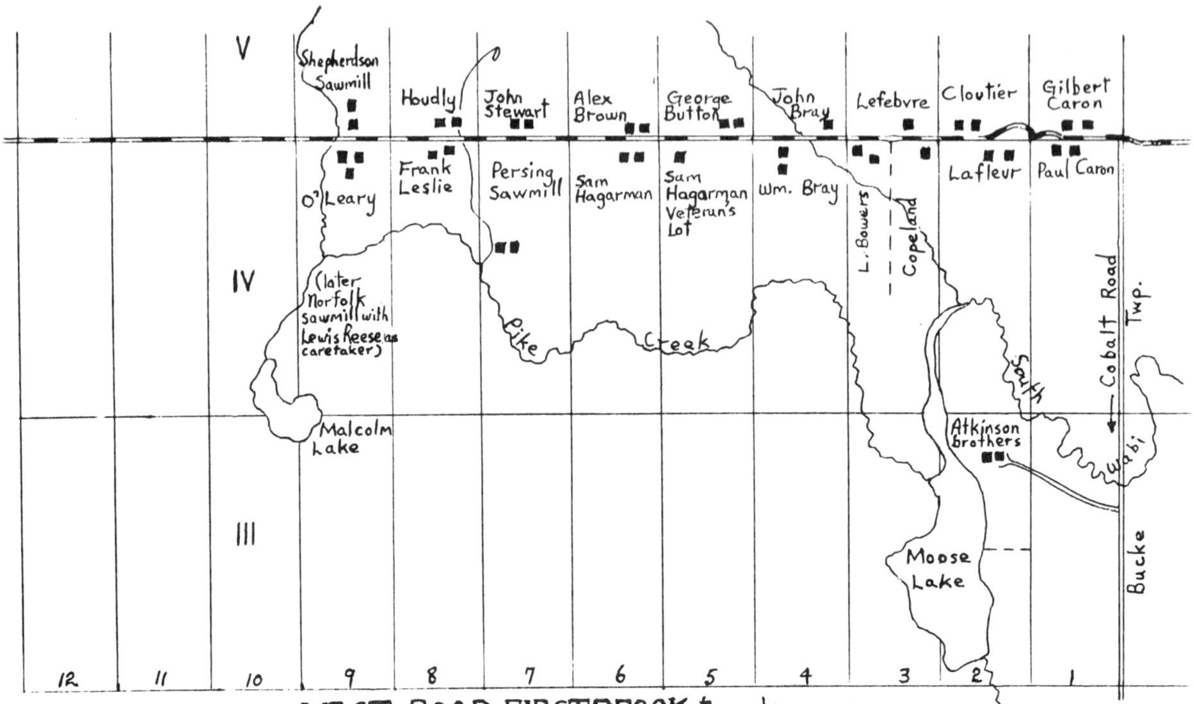

WEST ROAD, FIRSTBROOK township-c. 1914

Despite this summer's rain, the T.&N.O. has surveyed an extension of its Porcupine branch line to the Great Lakes port of Sault Sté. Marie. Southwest across Mattagami Lake at Wawaitin Falls the line would connect with the Canadian Northern railway at Conden, fifty-three miles from Timmins. Few clay slides would threaten a rail line along this route, for the survey party had described a rough country of lake-studded rock. Without a trace of minerals, though. Now the Commission must decide whether to spend $22,000 a mile to open up country which may not sustain a mine, let alone a farm.

What of this season's other survey of a rail line from Cochrane to James Bay? Long an Ontario dream, the mouth of Moose River would give the province an ocean port. And the line would give access to vast lignite coal deposits along the way. Oil? Diamonds?

On a hunting trip this fall, F.H. Anson of Ogilvie Flour Mills started dreaming when he reached Iroquois Falls. After last summer's forest fires destroyed thousands of New Ontario pulp wood acres, the McCormick's of Chicago grew nervous about this wild country. Yet confident of Abitibi River's immense hydro power and the measureless tract of still unspoilt timber Anson has bought their Iroquois Falls site and is now designing his own Pulp and Paper Company plans.

Unhappy workmen, however, might cause him to reconsider. At the other Porcupine end of the branch line, on November 15, the Western Federation of Miners calls a strike at McIntyre Mine. Angry at a reduction in their hourly wages, the men are demanding an eight hour day and a twenty-five to fifty percent wage raise. But the cash-poor company pleads it needs more time to find paying ore. And reasons, moreover, the demands are excessive compared to the standards set by Cobalt's mines:

Classification.	Average pay per 9-hour shift.
Shift Bosses	$4.00 to $5.00
Timbermen	3.25
Pumpmen	3.25
Machine drillers	3.25
Machine helpers	2.75
Machine drillers in wet shafts	3.50
Machine helpers in wet shafts	3.50
Hand drillers	2.75
Cage tenders	2.50
Trammers	2.50
Pipe fitters	2.75
Engineers	.30 an hour
Firemen	.25 "
Deck tenders	2.50
Surface labourers	2.25
Blacksmith	3.25 to $4.00
Blacksmith helper	2.50
Ore sorter	2.25
Carpenter	3.25

A deduction of 60c. per day is made for board, and $1.00 per month for hospital and doctor's fees.

Regardless of Cobalt's wage rates, the union argues, the price Porcupine's gold mines will soon receive for their highgrade ore will far exceed the price for Cobalt's silver. That youthful Hollinger Mine, in December, declares annual earnings of $933,682 promises a most profitable future. And since its mill is earning a weekly net profit of $40,000, the company on November 2 started paying its shareholders a three percent dividend every four weeks.

Although Cobalt's total mineral production has declined from last year's peak, prosperous life continues in the three main Temiskaming towns. Now the Nipissing Central trolley cars can clang over ten miles from Cobalt through Argentite, North Cobalt, Haileybury, Moore's Cove to New Liskeard where Lester Neil's drugstore has started selling return tickets. From the Vendome Hotel along the east side of LakeShore Road the Nipissing Central extension goes north to merge with the T.&N.O. spur at the foot of Florence Street. Sharing use of a common line north to Moore's Cove the trolley cars then switch on to one of the two main line tracks, leased from the T.&N.O. At the south limit of New Liskeard they switch back to their own company's right of way along LakeShore Road.

McKinley-Darragh-Savage orehouse

LakeShore Road, Haileybury, in foreground Jory's front lawn
Left to right: Mrs. Emma Jory with son John, Mrs. Jeanette Hamilton with Jean Jory

Eager to eliminate Nipissing Central's "back-door" Argentite Street terminus in Cobalt, especially because of the dangerous overpass at Argentite, the T.&N.O. Commission plans another lease of the second main line track so trolley cars can travel from North Cobalt directly to the comforts of Cobalt station. To its summer flower garden, its *Canada Railway News Company* newspaper, magazine and book stand, its ticket office, its elegant Brussel's carpet covering the waiting room floor and its few broad, outside steps up to the mid-town bustle of Cobalt Square. Where, for now, only charred timbers lump together what was once the Opera House before this summer's June 5 fire. And the black cavity extends back to where flames consumed Galoska's equipment building on Presley Street and the Cobalt Hotel on Commission Street. So distraught are some of the surviving businessmen, Tommy Black has paid a bargain price to buy the Imperial Hall building at the Square end of Lang Street for a hardware store. Just north of him is Peter Pano's Olympia candy store. Good reason Peter has to be still nervous, for only a few doors up the street is the wooden butcher shop whose wall still carries scorch marks from the 1909 fire.

Already, though, the town having paid John Martin $5,250 in October for his Cobalt Hotel site has plans to build a market place and curling rink there. And rumour has it the Wallaces will rebuild on their Opera House site.

But better to prevent fires than to plan rebuilding after them, Haileybury's fire chief Ike Quinn warned Mayor McAulay, as they toured in August an abandoned paper-strewn building on Broadway Street. First used as the mining recorder's original 1905 office this building became home to the semi-weekly *Silver City News.* After this Haileybury newspaper dropped its circulation to a weekly printing then stopped altogether, the *Cobalt News-Herald* briefly stirred. The *Haileybury Record* lasted eight months while the most recent newspaper attempt, *The Porcupine Press,* lasted even less. Today the wooden building still stands in Haileybury across from the Stitt house, but cleaned of fire-feeding paper.

Few Cobalt sleighs make the trip to Haileybury but those, that do, leave by the Haileybury Road, now called Lang Street after the former mayor. With lakes frozen and snow piling deeper, most winter travellers ride the ploughed railway lines. And repainted in T.&N.O. colours of green and gold the Nipissing Central cars look like run-a-ways from the main line.

Icemakers at the local curling and hockey rinks have almost flooded thick enough surfaces for games to begin. Especially impatient are Haileybury's curlers. Even though trolley cars, since chairman Englehart and commissioner Dane rode the first official car on October 23, can finally reach New Liskeard, Haileybury now has its own four sheets of pebbled ice in the new market building. And more men are joining the club. For twenty-five dollars a month the Temiskaming Trading Company does lease forty feet of the building's south end, and thirty rental stalls for farm produce do divide up the rest of the interior during the summer; but once November arrives, the sawdust floor is cleared for curling.

Interior of Cobalt T.&N.O. Station

Since his Silver Centre mine has closed, curler Bob Jowsey now lives in Haileybury and prospects for Noah Timmins. A busy practice affords dentist Joe Crawford curling nights off. But whether he will also curl this winter bothers Haileybury's other dentist, Dr. William R. Somerville. He and his bride have just moved into one of Kingswell's Main Street bungalows, between Magistrate Siegfried Atkinson's house and Alof Carlson's bungalow to the west. Jogging from his dentist's chair during the day to his new household at night he may not have the energy left to sweep a curling stone. In charge of Haileybury's Temiscaming Telephone office, Milt Boyd has free time, however. So does young Emmett Smith. This may be his first year as a curler but if he has any of the hockey or baseball finesse of his older brother Leonard, he should soon be skipping a rink.

Although George Taylor, president of the Temiscaming Telephone Company, and Jake Englehart, Chairman of the T.&N.O. Commission, signed a contract on November 8 to exchange local and long distance calls through their separate systems, Milt Boyd's Haileybury office will have no extra work. The agreement only affects Temiscaming Telephone offices at Cobalt and Englehart, which are now connecting circuits to the T.&N.O. offices for long distance calls. Accepting all local requests, the T.&N.O. Commission will pay the telephone company twenty-five percent of net receipts for its long distance conversations.

Despite Cobalt's silver production having declined this 1912 year by a million and a half ounces, the metal's increasing market price has improved annual profits by a million dollars. And because of the seven cent price rise, several abandoned properties have been reopened. And matching Seneca-

Superior's bonanza discovery at Cart Lake, the Casey Cobalt Mine, nine miles northeast of New Liskeard, has found a million ounces of silver ore. Enough to build its own reduction mill. Also with a new mill and its shaft now down over 700 feet through Keewatin greenstones into the diabase sill, the Beaver Mine in southeast Coleman township is finding "good milling values...along with some rich ore." Deeper than any in the Cobalt, South Lorrain and Gowganda districts, this exploratory Beaver shaft might well reveal the future direction of silver mining in Northern Ontario. After it reaches the Keewatin rock beneath the sill.

High and low prices of stocks of Cobalt-Silver Mines

Name of Company.	To end of 1907		1908		1909		1910		1911		1912	
	High	Low	High	Low	High	Low	High	Low	High	Low	High	Low
Beaver or Beaver Consolidated Mines, Limited..	.88	.20	.66½	.24	.44	.9¼	.38½	.18	.52	.25½	.50	.39
Buffalo Mines, Limited..........................	5.00	.80	3.62½	2.15	3.60	2.50	2.50	1.96	2.30	1.40	2.50	1.20
City of Cobalt Mining Company, Limited....	2.83	2.38	2.80	1.75	2.81	.33	.55½	.19½	.21	.05½	.36¼	.07
Cobalt Central Mines Company..............	.76	.16½	.74	.21	.58½	.24	.23	.06	.10	.01	.01	.0½
Cobalt Lake Mining Company, Limited......	.85	.09	.25¼	.10	.19½	.11½	.29¾	.12¼	.29¾	.12¾	.59	.17
Cobalt Silver Queen, Limited................	3.50	.62	1.28	.731	1.00	.19	.23	.04½	.10	.02	.07½	0.03
Coniagas Mines, Limited	8.50	3.30	7.20	3.90	7.00	5.25	6.00	4.19	7.60	6.00	8.25	6.70
Crown Reserve Mining Company, Limited....	3.10	.20	2.88	.38	5.99	2.63	4.10	2.52	3.60	2.38	3.60	2.00
Foster Cobalt Mining Company, Limited.....	4.37	.35	.89	.38	.70½	.22	.31	.04	.07	.02½	.19½	.03
Kerr Lake Mining Company, Limited	7.80	2.55	7.80	2.60	9.43	7.60	11.00	6.00	7.75	2.70	3.15	2.53
La Rose Consolidated Mines Company.......	.....	.....	7.12½	6.08	8.47	4.20	5.02	3.30	5.00	3.70	4.01	2.16
McKinley Darragh Savage Mines of Cobalt, Ltd.	4.12	.64½	1.20	.64½	1.01	.84	1.40	.79½	1.88	1.29	2.20	1.69
Nipissing Mines Company.....................	31.25	5.50	12.637	6.12	12.91	9.25	11.75	9.50	11.25	6.60	9.35	5.78
Right of Way Mining Company, Limited .. / The Right of Way Mines, Limited	10.50	1.00	4.00	3.65	3.70	1.30	.31	.20	.29¾	.04½	.13	.05
Temiskaming and Hudson Bay Mining Company, Limited .. / The Hudson Bay Mines, Limited	.....	.....	.....	.....	290.	148.	143.	98.	108.	80.	90.	63.
Temiskaming Mining Company, Limited.....	2.25	.26	2.00	.28½	1.79	.67	.98	.52	.92	.25½	.49	.30
Trethewey Silver Cobalt Mine, Limited	2.85	.46	1.80	.47	1.61	1.29	1.45	1.13½	1.22	.51	.77	.31
Wettlaufer-Lorrain Silver Mines, Limited	.....	.....	.....	.....	.....	.....	1.42	.52	1.23	.75	.83	.23

In his paper, "Recent Underground Development Work at Cobalt", read on March 7 at the annual Canadian Institute of Mining meeting at Toronto, Charles O'Connell reviewed Cobalt's history. "This district," he said, "is without a peer on the continent. The proved ore-bearing zone is a rectangle five by three miles, and from within this zone there has been produced in seven years to January 1, 1912, 126,064,189 ounces of silver...worth $64,918,752." Then O'Connell describes the rectangle:

Since the year 1906 the extent of the proved ore-bearing zone has not been enlarged. The limit is marked on the south and the east by the Temiskaming mine, on the west by the Princess, and on the north by the Hudson Bay. The district west of the town of Cobalt extending to Portage Bay has been prospected, but no productive veins have yet been found. The properties on what is termed the "West Ridge" extending from the Hudson Bay on the north to the Buffalo on the south, have been especially consistent producers. This is largely accounted for by the multiplicity of veins in the Huronian formation along the Ridge.

Taking a line from the Hudson Bay through the Trethewey, Coniagas, and Buffalo mines, there are, I would venture to say, in this area, more than eighty known productive veins. These largely belong to the main vein system traversing east and west, from which innumerable branches lead. The Trethewey property alone, from the main vein system near the south end of the property, has twenty-two productive veins. Some of these are branches from the main vein system, which strikes east. It will doubtless interest all mining engineers and geologists to know that only four of these veins showed a marked outcrop on the surface. More than six do not come closer to the surface than 50 feet.

McKinley-Darragh stope work

Cobalt's Future? "The immense quantity of milling ore which is to be extracted," O'Connell continues, "leads to the belief that the maximum number of tons per annum will not be reached for several years. ...Ten years would not be too long a period to estimate as the future minimum life of Cobalt."

And what about the discovery of new highgrade deposits? On October 11, Seneca-Superior Silver Mines' crosscut on the 200 foot level of its lease under Cart Lake broke into another calcite vein's four inch wide shoot of solid silver. After 200 feet of drifting, the vein shoot shows no signs of weakening.

In his own speech on Cobalt's future, at the March C.I.M. meeting Joseph B. Tyrell talked of an even longer life. Because the flat-lying diabase sill which originally penetrated Cobalt's Keewatin rock and mantle of conglomerate formed silver bearing veins in surrounding cracks as it cooled, why not explore all the surviving rocks which circled the sill? According to G.R. Mickle's pessimistic calculations in a paper, "Probable Silver Production of Cobalt", delivered on May 1 to the Cobalt branch of the C.I.M., eighty percent of Cobalt's 111 known productive veins occur in the brittle conglomerate remnants left exposed beneath where the diabase sill eroded away. But Tyrell has dared to speculate about Beaver Mine following a vein fissure down through the sill to the harder Keewatin rock, farther below, "I should not be at all surprised if in years to come, after the prospecting in the Cobalt camp is completed, the rocks beneath the diabase would produce as much, area for area, as those properties which have yielded so much silver in the past."

4

THEY CALL BACK TO US
- 1913 -

Through the spruce bush east of Swastika, Walter Little and sawmill partner Fred Douglas have finished cutting a broader trail to the west end of Kirkland Lake. Already Walter's team of oxen has sledded bagged Tough-Oakes' ore out to the T.&N.O. station for shipment to an American smelter which pays $1400 for the two tons. Next summer, to avoid two more miles of rugged road Walter will raft on canoes the Tough-Oakes' ore across the lake to the present road end.

ROYAL MAIL TEAM STARTING FOR KIRKLAND LAKE GOLD FIELDS, SWASTIKA, ONT.

Walter Little Royal Mail team starting for Kirkland Lake goldfields, Swastika, Doig's Store behind. Walter Little astride far ox. Mrs. Ernie Martin at rear in fur coat and hat, Mike Hackett at right foreground.

Harry Oakes has left the minesite for Cobalt where he is trying to interest Tom Jones, manager of the Buffalo Mine, to invest some money in Kirkland Lake. Yet just as cautious as three years ago when he refused taking an option on Porcupine's Dome Mine, Buffalo president Charlie Denison quickly advises, "No!". On to Haileybury, Harry goes. Clem Foster, the Tough brothers have told him, might help promote interest. Having contracted haulage work three years ago at his Mann Mine prospect at Gowganda, the Toughs well know his brokerage skills. And ever since he sold his mine at Cobalt, Clem Foster has banked much money of his own. Much like other local mining men, enough to attract this month the famous Sarah Bernhardt in the role of Queen Elizabeth at Cobalt's Empire Theatre.

Haileybury - Harry Holland, Bob Young, Alex Gillies, Weldon Young

At this same January time, Haileybury prospector Bob Jowsey, on his way back from a trip to Lake Kienawisik on the Harricanaw River for Noah Timmins' syndicate, steps off the train at Swastika. On the track siding beside the station is a carload of lumber George Tough, along with John Martin of Cobalt, is having Walter Little haul into the Tough-Oakes minesite for a hotel. Jowsey's curiosity increases at Boisvert's Hotel when he greets the familiar face of Albert Wende, of Buffalo, New York, who three years ago was managing the Bulldog Mine in South Lorrain for a group of Americans and whom Weldon Young has now persuaded to inspect Bill Wright's property. Weldon whose brother Robert died in the Cheddite plant explosion at Haileybury last October is not able to accompany him. So together, before daybreak, Jowsey and Wende snowshoe Little's bush trail northeast. Three hours later spying Bill Wright's campfire smoke at the far end of the lake they tramp over the snow crusted ice to his tent for a warm plate of breakfast pancakes. Hefting a gold flecked sample from Wright's discovery vein, Jowsey wonders aloud whether he is too late for a share of Kirkland Lake ground. Not yet! Haileybury plumber McKane's claim may be for sale, Wright's British Army accent barks. Leaving Wende to his own thoughts, Jowsey this afternoon speeds back to spend the night at Boisvert's Swastika Hotel. But before checking in he first goes to the T.&N.O. station to telephone Union Bank manager George Bagshaw at Haileybury to ask McKane for a price. First thing tomorrow he will walk down Main Street and negotiate a payment of $3,555. Finally at home on Georgina Avenue just north of Probyn Street across from fellow prospector Stodhart Forneri's house, he wonders again if this Kirkland Lake property will prove more profitable than their former Silver Centre claims. No regrets, though. Now he and his newest partners must raise public money and start another search for minerals. Since Charlie Richardson, one of the partners in this latest syndicate, is not in his house farther north on Georgina, Bob wires him in Toronto to visit Queen's Park and secure the name Kirkland Lake for a company title.

Also in Toronto is George Turk, pastor of Haileybury's Central Methodist Church. On Tuesday afternoon, February 4, he marries Minda Huntington of Toronto who can now look forward to moving back to Haileybury where she formerly lived. For her, the town's new Methodist church sounds more exciting than any remote mineral prospect farther up the T.&N.O. line, than anything up north.

Yet interested in extending the Nipissing Central line further north, the *New Liskeard Speaker,* in its February 7 issue, insists the Ontario government "at the earliest possible date" should open its eyes to the immense traffic potential between New Liskeard and North Temiskaming; at least do something, the newspaper suggests, instead of today's dithering over whether to build a railway bridge or an ordinary wagon one across Blanche River.

Look to your own eyesight, Queen's Park answers New Liskeard's spokesman. Look to Mr. Leng, for example, who wants town help. On February 3, along with Messrs McFarlane and Chester of Dymond township, he appeared at the town council meeting to complain about overflow from the town's standpipe washing gulley-deep ditches across their farmlands. And while New Liskeard corrects its reservoir's water level, Mr. Leng asks, what about also linking the west end of Whitewood Avenue to the town's sewage system?

Certainly New Liskeard now feels confident enough to do so. For construction has finally begun on its government dock. Representing contractors McCool and Moffatt of Pembroke, Frank Fortin has George Peters superintending the entire job. Working off Wabis River's two foot ice thickness, sub-contractor Faralley is driving 500 piles cut by Grant and Kennedy's local sawmill west of town. After he finishes this by July, timber for the 60 x 120 foot dock with its 32 x 36 foot approach will bolt into place. Over a hundred wagon loads of gravel will raise ground level over the old Wabi Foundry site to the wharf. Then a 40 by 70 foot freight shed with two offices will handle the transfer of goods from lake boats to spur line train. Although Lumsden's dock, some 200 feet to the north, will remain, there will be ample room between old and new for several large ships. Yet the *New Liskeard Speaker* is suspicious: How long will Faralley's jack pine piles last? Why was water resistant cedar or tamarac not used? The T.&N.O. has always frowned on jack pine ties; if anyone had bothered to ask, the Commission could tell many railway tie stories of this wood's fast decay.

Perhaps, though, the Commission was too busy completing last minute details on its branch line to Elk Lake. And then there was the fuss over the opening afternoon ceremony on February 4. Rushing construction of the 26 x 73 foot station with its 12 foot wide, 95 foot long platform, the T.&N.O. work crew which had taken over final completion of the line had to make sure station agent O. Belanger and his staff would royally welcome all first arrivals. As chairman Englehart and fellow commissioners stepped down from their special car on the first passenger train they faced Elk Lake's reeve A.H. Porter and councillors who, under a "triumphal arch" between the bank building and Porter's store, presented the chairman with a key to the "city". Made out of native silver from Beaver Auxiliary Mine, the eighteen inch long key weighed more than three pounds. Against Jake Englehart's heavy fur coat the polished beaver clinging to a wreath of maple leaves on the key's handle glistened as if it had just been born. After hammering the silvered last spike, chairman Englehart and his companions that clear, bright Tuesday bundled aboard a sleigh to tour Beaver Mine. And a return for 5:00 o'clock dinner in the Flat Iron building where, when slivers started to rise later from the Masonic dance floor, the T.&N.O. commissioners finally retired to their train for sleep and tomorrow's departure, back over tracks by three stations chief T.&.N.O. engineer Clement has named after favourite characters in Longfellow's poem, *Hiawatha.*

That the former railhead of Charlton would lose business did keep the festive celebration from bragging too loudly about Elk Lake's future prosperity. Just how much will Charlton shrink? Can it continue to support two post offices? postmaster Herbert Quinn asks his wife Charlotte. Theirs is on the east side of Blanche River; Tom Fowke's is on the other side next to the railway station. Let alone the possible demise of Fowke's and Gerrard's general store, how can Jim Coles, Narcisse Legault, H.S. Malkin, Jim Morrison, Miller and McDonnell hope their hardware, grocery, furniture and lumber businesses stay alive? William Laurence delivers the Charlton mail but what livery stable assurance will Harry Hill and his son have when the old Charlton to Elk Lake winter road drifts into disuse? What about my Beaver Board Timber Company? H. Douglas asks. And which people will move away? public school principal Ben Bolton, and teacher Violet Roberts want to know. Teaching at the separate school, Pearle Ryther is just as anxious. After next Sunday's Presbyterian and Methodist services the ministers promise one another to talk of joining congregations. In five years time there may be barely enough people left for one church.

Just as *The Charlton Advance* describes how the power plant being built by Northern Ontario Light and Power Company will send 33,000 volts on a twenty-six mile transmission line to Kirkland Lake, Charlton, like Latchford today, may not need much power itself. Kalil Farah had first converted Ryan's old saw mill at the east side of the Falls. Then three years ago, Smith and Fawcett bought its hydro powered dynamo. Now with the new dam and its powerful flume, Charlton's townspeople can only take heart its voltage will provide a paying future in developing Kirkland Lake. A longer future, they hope, than the short-lived time the town spent making quick money as the railhead departure point for Elk Lake and Gowganda's mines.

Yet sending Charlton power out will not bring customers in, hotel man Paul Dagenais moans. From its peak of two hotels, five churches, two post offices, four meeting halls, twelve stores, a bakery, a Union Bank branch office, three blacksmiths, a tinsmith, a railway station with sixteen switches in its yard and a dock on Long Lake, Charlton could crumble into ghost town dust. And will medical doctor George Cooper stay? L. McGugan still manages the T.&N.O. telephone exchange at the station with Ida Stewart as operator, but for how much longer?

Even the town of Elk Lake may not prosper too long if another fire like the February 5 one that destroyed the Smyth riverfront buildings happens again. Whipped by 6:00 o'clock blizzard winds the morning flames did $40,000 worth of damage to the Matabanick Hotel, the Fire Hall and Hose Tower, the Lang-Jodouin building, the Gowganda Trading Company building, the Hudson's Bay store, the Ontario Steamboat Company building, Assaf's dry goods store, a Chinese laundry and restaurant, J.R. Booth's office, A.M. Daniels' division court clerk's office and the Military Stores. Dying in the hotel heat were prospector Edward O'Keefe, miner Robert Sovie and William Wilkinson, a watchman at the Merriman camps downriver. Jack Fraser, the hotel's bartender injured himself when he jumped for his life from the balcony. And hotel owner Asa Ribble saved himself, his wife and daughter Louise, but not before pounding on the hallway doors of sleeping guests and leading them outside. As T.&N.O. chairman Englehart's private railway car, *Sir James,* pulled out of the nearby station this same morning the snowstorm blinded any view of black smoke but the wood ash smell raged after the train down river.

Rely on your area farmers, the T.&N.O. Commission counsels Charlton: agriculture will thrive decades after the mines have come and gone; you have a railway line; use it to ship your produce south.

Happier with the shifting fortunes of New Ontario are lumbermen A.J. Murphy and Matt Conkey of Haileybury. Cutting burnt-over jack pine, small stands of white and red pine on the old Booth Limits during the last three years they can now build a saw mill at Murphy's Siding on the new T.&N.O. branch to Elk Lake. Then much more quickly will their Montreal River logs move to market as sized lumber. Matt Conkey who owned mineral claims in South Lorrain and a share of Haileybury's Maple Leaf Hotel, now prefers the steady profitable business of logging timber. Though Arthur Murphy financed the Maidens Silver Mine in South Lorrain, lumbering has always been his preferred livelihood.

Even though they will first float today's logs part way down the Montreal River, A.J. no longer fears another mess like the freakish January thaw in 1900 when Booth's logs he had piled on Mill Creek east of North Cobalt suddenly began floating on the flood of melting snow over the ice down to the rocky corner where Farr's sawmill once stood, and tangled upwards into a fifty foot high Chinese puzzle.

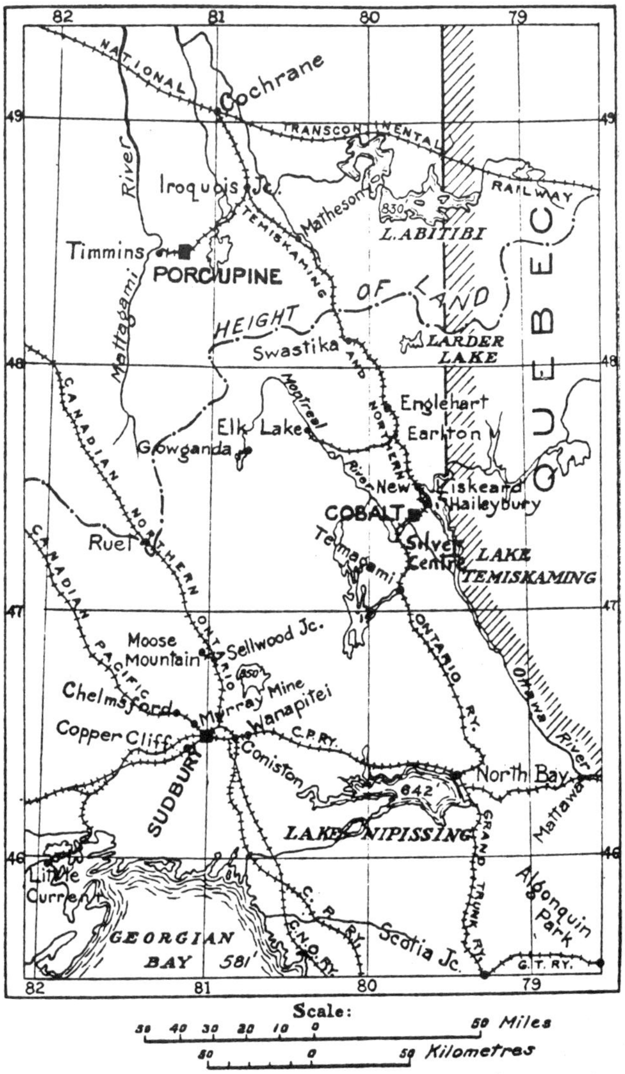

Index map of the Cobalt-Porcupine-Sudbury region.

Having first made mineral money in South Lorrain Bob Jowsey is eager to mine more from the scarcely scratched surface of Kirkland Lake. On February 25, he and his Haileybury syndicate friends incorporate McKane's claim as Kirkland Lake Gold Mines, the first mining company to stamp an official name on Teck township ground. Slower are Bill Wright, Harry Oakes and the Tough brothers; but with a few recently earned Tough-Oakes dollars for dynamite, beans and rice, Harry is back at Kirkland Lake with Ernie Martin and two miners privately handsteeling the lakeside shaft. In bitter cold they pile highgrade from a narrow shoot and snare rabbits for their stew pot. Tired of scouring other rocks around the world, Harry is so sure he has finally found his own mine, he pledges to bury his starved bones here if he is mistaken. Especially fatalistic he is since his father's death three weeks ago at Dover, Maine.

Glad Harry Oakes is to have Ernie Martin's personal help. For at McIntyre Porcupine Mine, underground workers have paraded strike signs on surface since last fall. Fistfights have spilled so much blood in Timmins the mayor has had to read the Riot Act. To protect surface equipment and the few miners still on company pay, McIntyre has hired four guards from the Thiel Detective Agency who in recent panic fired their guns at the pressing picketers—wounding three. Demanding justice the local union immediately appealed to Magistrate Atkinson of Haileybury to hold court. In summary conviction he fined each detective $100 for assault. Having had his jurisdiction extended, a year ago this May 13, to cover all of Temiskaming, Nipissing and Sudbury districts the magistrate promises to impose even stiffer fines and sentences on anyone else who breaks the law. The McIntyre workers may have found courtroom justice; but having failed to persuade Cobalt miners to call a sympathy strike and aching from hunger, they are now asking for their jobs back. Only on our terms, the mineowners reply.

If cash-poor McIntyre Mine had not surprisingly cut the miners' wages, the labour strike would probably never have happened. And the men would have been as peaceful as any of those in Cobalt who on Monday, March 17, jam Nipissing Central trolley cars north to watch a picked team of hockey players from the Cobalt Mine League and Haileybury battle New Liskeard's town team. As the *Speaker* reports on Friday, "Cliff Burkholder's New Liskeard boys defeated the Haileybury All Stars eleven goals to nine. The locals had it over the Stars when it came to combination play, and this is exactly where the boys from the Farmer's town won their game." Chasing players up and down the ice both referee Harry Woodhouse and judge-of-play Ace Jewell almost collapsed from exhaustion.

Cobalt Comet (Drummond) Mine, Kerr Lake, Coleman township, Dr. Drummond's house at centre top

Encouraged by such a sports victory, the *New Liskeard Speaker,* on April 25, feels bold enough to reopen the District Judicial Seat debate: since Haileybury has still not decided on a site for the courthouse "we would suggest to the Honorable, the Minister of Public Works, that the Liskeard offer still holds good,...Haileybury is not the only pebble." A week later, as an alternative to the originally selected Ferguson Avenue public school grounds, C.C. Farr offers for $8,000 his original seven Haileybury homestead location lots at the northeast corner of Main Street and Georgina Avenue. Tim Marleau has agreed to vacate the lower floor rooms he rents for his real estate office. Immediately the government signs the order to demolish Haileybury's first building.

The April 16 sale of the Drummond family's mine to Cobalt Comet Mines had already reminded Tri-Town people that old energies inevitably give way to new ones. A more local reminder this was than Jim Hughes' April 8 purchase of John Reamsbottom's claims at the west end of Kirkland Lake and incorporation of Teck-Hughes Gold Mines. Yet not so threatening: anxious were the first conversations about Porcupine, and now they focus on Kirkland Lake. How much longer before both these gold areas take centre stage from Cobalt's aging mines?

Ice-breaking another Temiskaming winter behind on Saturday, April 26, Captain Ladouceur docks the steamer *Aileen* at New Liskeard and on Monday begins his regular local trips to Haileybury, Guiges, North Temiskaming and New Liskeard. As soon as the smaller *Zara* leaves dry dock it can carry extra freight. Especially since twelve additional feet have increased its length and three more feet its width. With the new control dam at the foot of Lake Temiskaming holding high water levels, steamer captains entering the mouth of the Wabis need no longer fear running aground; but New Liskeard townspeople now fear their steel bridge is about to collapse. Washing clay banks away the higher water threatens to undermine concrete supports at the bridge's south end. Five thousand dollars worth of damage so far, town council charges: the federal government should be prepared to pay.

Despite the danger, people do cross the bridge next Saturday evening to hear music teacher Isabel Wilcox's pupils at the Sons of England Hall. The first real sign of spring this annual recital is, they say: for the boats have arrived on a high tide and the robins have yet to come. Surrounded by begonias and flags, introduced by Angus McKelvie and accompanied by Miss Wilcox's piano, Miss Young plays adult solos on her violin, Miss Ward follows with her mandolin, until Miss Murray's soprano voice finally fills the hall with "Sing On".

Fresh spring brings careless dreams. And a forgotten bonfire this same May evening almost destroys Englehart. After sweeping clean his Fourth Avenue bakery shop, S. Holditch set fire to the waste outside. Thinking its smoking embers would smother themselves, he left the pile to darkness. Yet at four o'clock Sunday morning a light breeze fanned sparks onto roof shingles of the adjoining building. While flames roared, the fire brigade rode the bucking pumper engine until its water trickled dry. Kert's King Edward Hotel did escape damage as well as a stretch of buildings from there to Kennedy's Hotel beside the railway station. And somehow others on the street facing the railway tracks also survived. But by nine o'clock in the morning the fire had wiped out thirty stores—most of Englehart's businesses, Mayor Henry O'Grady mourns.

Thankful is Englehart's Dr. Lowery that the fire caused no death or injuries. New Liskeard's Lady Minto Hospital may have a few beds available, but with Dr. Young just having moved to Toronto, the hospital is short of staff. Cobalt Mines hospital admits only local miners and their families. And Haileybury's Sisters of Providence hospital building is still without a roof. As soon as complete, though, the sisters promise their doors will open to all. And to make sure a Roman Catholic doctor will be there to comfort French speaking patients in their own language, Bishop Latulipe has arranged for twenty-five year old Hector Joyal, a recent medical graduate of Laval University, to move to Haileybury.

Englehart. T.&N.O. station in background, Kert's King Edward Hotel at right

Knowing Bishop Latulipe would prefer living closer to his cathedral church, the Temiskaming Roman Catholic congregation has continually urged a Bishop's Palace be built in Haileybury. But this will mean a move from his present palace beside George Taylor's LakeShore Road house in New Liskeard. Diocese business, however, demands almost daily appearances at the central church in Haileybury.

Possibly the best location for the new palace is on the south side of the cathedral where the Sisters of Assumption operated their temporary convent. But the Cecil Street name of this proposed site, at this June moment, may mean more in Kirkland Lake than here in Haileybury, for its namesake English mining engineer Henry Cecil recently signed an option to purchase many of Kirkland Lake's claims.

Attracted by the telluride content of Tough-Oakes' highgrade ore, Cecil believes surrounding ground will be just as fertile. Already he is visiting England to sell his Burnside options. And he can mention that neighbouring Tough-Oakes Gold Mines has taken a confident step forward with its June 12 incorporation, that Bob Fennell of Haileybury has assured Tough-Oakes president Clem Foster he can sell enough stock to pay for a five-stamp mill beside the shaft going down on number two vein. Meanwhile, mine manager Charles O'Connell and engineer M.W. Hotchkin are plotting the best underground way to break rock for the mill. Vice-president, Harry Oakes has a say, but to insure further his personal chances of success he has borrowed more money from his family in Maine to buy Robin's and Wright's two claims between Wright's discovery property and the Tough-Oakes' ground. And the day after Tough-Oakes' company birth, he incorporates these claims as Sylvanite Gold Mines with himself as president.

While Henry Cecil, in May, was carefully assessing the telluride evidence of gold highgrade at Kirkland Lake, Weldon Young signed a deal with Albert Wende of Buffalo to finance Bill Wright's property. Since he himself had previously paid $7,500 for Ed Hargreaves' share of the claims, Young was in a strong partnership position to negotiate. Now, though, impatient of delay he has cancelled the Buffalo deal and let the Cartwright brothers of Haileybury option a five eighth's interest. Wasting no time they have sent handsteeling miners from their Temiskaming Mine at Cobalt to start sinking a shaft on the discovery vein at the east end of Kirkland Lake.

Swastika

Swimmers at Haileybury, Ted Atkinson on left, 1913

With the Kirkland Lake windfall cash still swelling his Haileybury bank account, Ed Hargreaves recently considered buying Desrocher's Haileybury butcher shop at the southwest corner of Main Street and Rorke Avenue. Brother-in-law Bill Wright may have the bachelor freedom to stay in the bush but Ed has a wife, son and two young daughters wanting him to stay closer to home. Although successful with his house painting and decorating contracts, Ed wants a steadier business all year round. And why not return to the butcher trade he left behind in England?

Considering the plight of McIntyre Porcupine Mines, Ed Hargreaves can easily convince himself he is better off having sold his share of Kirkland Lake ground. On June 5, Albert Freeman resigned as president and director of McIntyre. Found guilty of stock promotion fraud in several United States mining schemes, he has been sentenced to five years in the penitentiary at Atlanta. So precarious are McIntyre's finances, by June 26 the company's new president Harley Curtis must use $10,000 of his own money to pay angry creditors. And his miners are not finding much gold. Yet why is neighbouring Hollinger Mine doubling its gold profits of last year? Noah Timmins suggests his miners are such decent men the ore shoots are finding them.

Not so long ago Cobalt's Kerr Lake and Crown Reserve mines enjoyed great vein wealth but now together they are pumping Kerr Lake dry so miners can stope out the last of their shared vein through to surface. And then what? Once the silver rich crown pillars are gone, Kerr Lake's water will seep back to flood the old underground workings, possibly forever.

A June discovery at the City of Cobalt Mine, however, shows not all old mine workings should be written off as finished. On one of their afternoon searches for hidden ore clues, resident manager Charles E. Watson and mine superintendent William F. Fancy stalked the unused second level workings north towards the Coniagas boundary. Ten feet short of the drift face, Cap Fancy detected specks of cobalt bloom inside a crack in the wall. Ordered to drill a crosscut there, machinemen after going thirty-five feet to the southeast intersected a four inch vein of smaltite. Blasting out one more round, they have found a strong seam of 1500 ounce silver ore.

Yet the discovery angers Frank Cody. When City of Cobalt president Shillington placed his company up for sale in January to an English syndicate, Frank Cody challenged the sale with a better offer of $900,000. Then several major shareholders sought a court injunction to cancel the English option. Too late, though; and having paid 55 cents a share the English syndicate may now own a bonanza.

McKinley-Darragh Mill, Cobalt

Make sure you photograph this latest silver discovery, local doomsayers preach, for it may be one of Cobalt's last. Alex MacLean of Haileybury has the camera equipment and would want the job but he must spend more time in his store selling sheet music, Nordheimer and Steinway pianos. And ever since Pauline Bagshaw, the Union Bank manager's wife, bought the first Steinway five minutes after it arrived in Haileybury, he has also decided to add Edison phonograph players to the display window of his studio in the Stitt House at 52 Broadway Street. Perhaps George A. Smith who has another studio down the street in the Jory and Young Block on Ferguson Avenue could photograph the discovery instead. Forget it, say Dan Essa and Tom Ross of Cobalt—either one of our Lang Street studios will do the job.

Amused by photographers pecking over grains of Tri-Town business, Leonard Hill and John Clark of New Liskeard have combined competing differences into a larger company with Frank Francis, the town's former assistant fire chief. About to purchase a small millworks plant towards the west end of Whitewood Avenue, the new partners are ready to do any construction job, anywhere, at any time. Having lost his arm in a cement mixer while bricking the new Imperial Bank's face at the northeast corner of Armstrong and Whitewood, Len Hill especially has proven his dedication to hard work.

Hill-Clark and Francis certainly need a wood milling plant today. On April 30 they began building Mark England's new twenty by thirty foot bake-shop, with concrete floor and foundation, on Pine Street. A baker from Chatham, Mark has moved here to build on his mother's property and form a partnership with brother Henry, presently working at Grills' store. With the bake-shop now complete, Mark's wife and son John have just arrived from Chatham to live in Ben Carruther's former house on Armstrong Street. Following close behind on June 24 Mr. Marsh of Toronto to build the bakery's eleven by twelve foot oven. The Englands' unmarried sister is already dusting clean a corner store in the McKelvie Block on Armstrong Street. At this location next to Nipissing Central's final stop, streetcar passengers will soon be able to buy her fresh breads, cakes and pastries before crossing the bridge for home.

With the England's job done, Hill-Clark and Francis are now preparing plans and materials for Cobalt's new 106 by 43 foot, three-storey municipal building. To be built on the charred site of the former Cobalt Hotel the new town hall will also contain a farmer's market on the ground floor facing the T.&N.O. station yard.

While New Liskeard's construction company may be willing to work all hours, many of the town's other businessmen feel years of past effort have earned them some summer's rest. In the *Speaker's* June 13 edition they announce: "We the undersigned merchants" will "close every Wednesday afternoon at one o'clock beginning June 25, 1913 and every Wednesday after until the end of August with exception of July 2: George Taylor Hardware, J. Redpath, W.H. Elliott and Company, L. Piche, Capling and Hickling, Wes McKnight, Gordon Davies Limited, J.F. Mulligan, The Grills Company, P. Woodward, A.J. Coombe, Thorpe Bros., C.F. Walkinshaw, J.W. Bolger, R.S. Robinson, I. Shaw, W.H. Beckett, Walton and Foster, Wm. Magladery, Mrs. MacDougall, A.P. Gervais, The Binkley Company, S. Greenwood, The Watson Company, John Leng, The Jamieson Meat Company."

Having proven his dedication to work in New Liskeard and Temiskaming, Kalil Farah is about to leave New Ontario. Since his recent acquittal from court charges of manipulating stock market prices in his Cobalt mines, he now looks forward to a less embarrassing, more restful life in the south. So on Thursday evening, June 26, a number of townspeople gather in The Liskeard Club to wish Kalil Farah a final goodbye. Tomorrow he goes south where "educational facilities are desirable for the growing members of his family." Mayor Kennedy hopes the gift of a goldheaded cane will not only support him but also jog memories of his many northern friends.

New Liskeard Bowling Champions, 1913

1. Jay Perrault
2. Jake Solomon
3. Bill Froggett
4. Ernie Frisby
5. _____
6. Sam Ritchie
7. Prescott Woodward

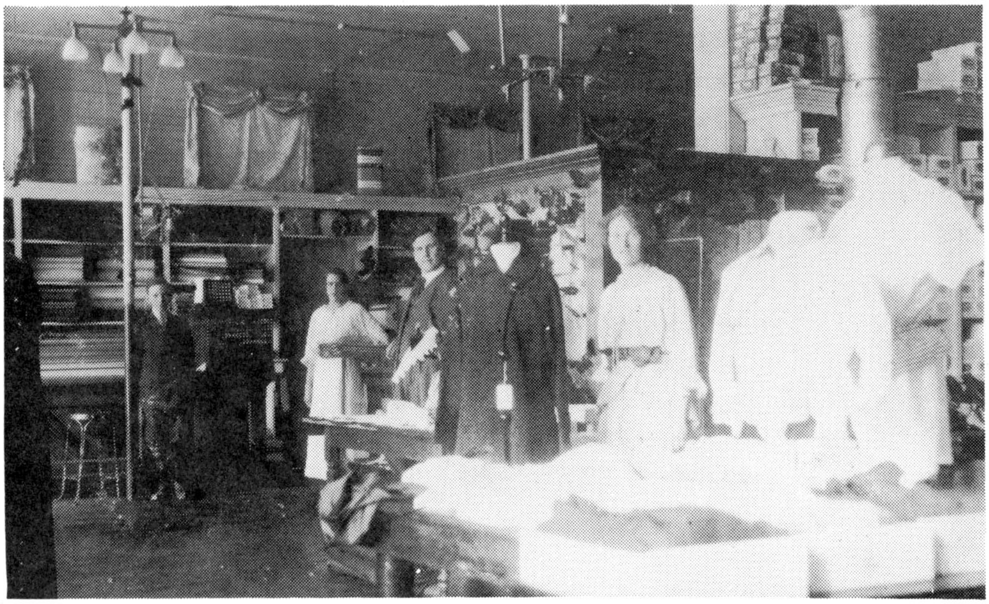

W.H. Elliott store interior, New Liskeard

In Temiskaming there seems to be as many social clubs as mines. Only recently William J. Hallett, Inspector of Public Schools, organized the Temiskaming Preceptory of the Masonic Order, the first one of its kind in the north. As first preceptor, he is holding Temple meetings in the former Presbyterian church building, now squeezed behind the new church on Haileybury's Browning Street. Most convenient for him as he and his wife Caroline live in the next house up the street.

Canada House across Wabis River bridge. Upper Ontario Steamboat Company building in viewer's left foreground - New Liskeard

Every Temiskaming town and village seems to have its own Orange Lodge. And on July 12 their members mass together in annual pilgrimage to Cochrane. Two excursion trains leave the local area, one picking up passengers from Latchford to Englehart, but not including Elk Lake. With the train leaving Latchford at five o'clock in the morning and New Liskeard forty-three minutes later, the long day of travel and parade might tire the Orangemen's sanctity but who can resist the low return railway fare of $3.45 from New Liskeard?

Seeing for themselves the bustle of prospectors at Swastika station and the shunting of freight cars at Iroquois Falls-Porcupine Junction, the Orangemen can believe the rumours coming out of Kirkland Lake of another mining camp like Porcupine. Had they not heard in April that Jim Hughes hired Sandy McIntyre to prospect his newly acquired Teck-Hughes property at the west end of Kirkland Lake; and that still feeling guilt over the stingy amount of money he had paid thirsty Sandy three years ago for a share of his Porcupine claim, Hughes has promised him a rich bonus for any gold discovery. Now, the story circulates, Sandy has found a vein which lines up with Wright's discovery at the far end of Kirkland Lake; so Jim Hughes has given him 150,000 shares of Teck-Hughes company stock.

Train over Blanche River bridge at Englehart

A half mile southwest the same vein seems to have been found at the bedrock bottom of a twenty foot trench in the northwest corner of Stephen Orr's claim. Continuing 300 more feet west another twenty foot deep hole down through the overburden on Kirkland Lake Gold Mines' property has revealed what must be another section of the vein. West again on Dave Elliott's claim prospectors are shovelling clear a heavy fracture zone along the same strike. Away from this long vein length, about three quarters of a mile over the hill south of where Sandy McIntyre has made the Teck-Hughes discovery, Jack Hunton, Tom Burt and Dan Whorley have dug up fistful nuggets of gold. So far without luck at the eastern side of Teck township, Jack Costello is tracing the Burnside vein's possible extension through Sylvanite Mines' property.

Still negotiating the sale of his Burnside option, Henry Cecil has installed a steam plant there. And he tells the adjoining Tough-Oakes owners that his possible buyers from London, England, especially H.G. Latilla, might also be willing to purchase a hefty amount of their company stock. Then eager to raise extra cash for underground development, Clem Foster prepares to set sail from New York. Meanwhile, Cecil with four geologists, Latilla has sent out from England, has started diamond drilling and mapping the Burnside acreage. With Ernie Martin taking more turns on the jackhammer, Harry Oakes, in free moments, is still slaving away at his nearby lakeshore exploration shaft. Closer by with more money and men, the Cartwrights' miners are copying his idea.

Sceptical of their Kirkland Lake option chances, Burr and Morgan Cartwright wonder whether their best bet may be millions of undiscovered silver ounces waiting under the diabase sill at their Temiskaming Mine near Cobalt. So they count the days until neighbouring Beaver Consolidated Mines completes sinking its shaft down through the sill to the unexplored Keewatin rock below. Other Coleman township mineowners like those of the Lumsden and Rochester working the same Keewatin-diabase on opposite Brady Lake shorelines also long for good news of silver. In Toronto at last year's Canadian Mining Institute meeting, Dr. Joseph B. Tyrell again emphasized the ore bearing silver solutions at Cobalt had "spread out laterally beneath the relatively impervious diabase sill and had descended into the fissures which had been formed by the subsequent cooling of the rocks beneath the diabase." And Casey Cobalt Mines' newly discovered highgrade deposit eight miles northeast of New Liskeard proves the persistent and thorough search of all likely mineral structures does pay. Extremely well, for this August, while the mine's two-stamp mill stands idly by, teamsters haul 825,000 bagged ounces of silver highgrade out to the T.&N.O. station at New Liskeard.

Lumsden Mining Company, Brady Lake, Coleman township;
Mines Power substation on background hill

Stowing their nets, however, out on Windy Point, around the east side of Dawson's Point commercial fishermen George and Peter Simmons of New Liskeard curse their hard times. After the T.&N.O. reached New Liskeard in 1905, the government had granted commercial licenses for gill net fishing. And for the last seven years fishermen have earned a summer and winter livelihood from selling locally scaled, dressed trout and pickerel for ten cents a pound, cheaper varieties for five cents. Any surplus catches they have sent packed in ice to New York city. But now Lake Temiskaming is closed to fishermen. Be patient until 1915, the government is telling them— by then depleted fish stocks will have had time to recover.

New Liskeard swimmers at Sharp's Landing

Difficult this closure is to understand for public school pupils in New Liskeard: many of their parents, like the Simmons brothers, depend on catching, buying or selling fish; if Lake Temiskaming is so broad, long and deep, why does the government stop their parents' business? Teachers from last year, Misses Weston, Laird, Ward and Mrs. Hull have resigned but their replacements Miss L. Gimby of Sault Ste. Marie, Miss Margaret Foster of Maynooth and Miss Delta Inglis of Englehart attempt to explain how more fish are being caught than hatched. Mr Hogarth, the principal, suggests some of the senior classes study the life cycle of fish; let the juniors draw pictures. Remaining on staff from last year, Misses Kate Menzies, Ida Higgins, Emily Young and Mr. E.W. Cornell believe they can soothe any fears, especially with Miss Young's accompanying violin.

New Liskeard Public School

New Liskeard's Separate School must do the soothing same, Miss McAlpine, the principal, tells her staff. Even though they are unhealthily cramped into too little classroom space. Two years ago the school's pupil population had grown so large the School Board moved most of the classes from the one room building on LakeShore Road to the Roman Catholic church. With the population still growing, Separate School Board members this year, J.O. O'Grady, J. Wadsworth, E. Donald, C.S. Delisle, J.W. Bolger, W.J. Yates and J.F. Mulligan have bought three corner lots at LakeShore Road and Dymond Crescent. Next year no one will remember the tangle of burdock, thistle and devil's paintbrush which blanketed the field where the new school is to stand.

Meteor steaming into Haileybury dock

Similarly cramped and wanting healthy family space the McDonough brothers have moved from Porcupine to Haileybury. Their worry about Patrick and Michael, ill all last winter with typhoid fever, started the move. That Eddie graduated in June from Cochrane Public School and can next attend Haileybury High School completed it. Rooted in Golden City since 1910 and prospecting their Porcupine claims throughout the summer fires of 1911, the brothers joined last year's rush into Kirkland Lake to stake more than 1,000 acres in Lebel township. Now, Charles, Peter, Patrick, Joseph, John, Michael, Albert, Edmond and Timothy may enjoy a permanent home near where their sister Mary has settled down in North Cobalt, married to Neil McIsaac, a Nipissing Central conductor. And Joe can use the central location as headquarters for his latest job as chief prospector for Fred Connell. Young Eddie and Tim will continue their schooling.

Five years ago the nine brothers and one sister had lived in Cobalt. With their parents close to death from fever in 1906 at the Maniwaki homestead in Quebec, they joined together in the booming silver town where Joe had waited on enough tables at Buffalo Mines' dining hall to deserve a promotion to head cook at the Beaver Mine, while Pete and Patrick worked underground. So today not finding anything of mineral value on their Kirkland Lake claims, the older brothers plan to drop them, stay in Haileybury, work in the Cobalt mines, cut mine timber and continue prospecting until they "strike it rich."

Rather than abandon their Kirkland Lake property, though, the Hughes brothers have hired Jack Hammell to find a buyer for their Teck-Hughes Mine. Quickly contacting Sam Cohen of Cobalt's Crown Reserve Mine, just as he did for Barney McEneny's Porcupine claim two years ago, Hammell must wait until Cohen's engineers finish their close sampling of assay values. But this time they report a property not worth buying. And help shroud Kirkland Lake in September gloom.

Regardless, Henry Cecil still has his four English engineers diamond drilling the Burnside ground. And H.G. Latilla, of London, England, who had advanced Cecil enough money to install the steam plant, has said he will buy as much Kirkland Lake mining land as he can if the drill core promises a deepening wealth of gold. But for now he dares not risk optioning and spending more money on the area.

Earlier in London this summer he did listen to Clem Foster's glowing description of the Tough Oakes' vein, next to the Burnside ground. And after handling the weight of several gold chunks Foster had brought to England, Latilla agreed to buy a million shares of Tough-Oakes' stock at forty cents a share. With presidential power of attorney, Clem Foster hastily signed the deal. And just as hastily Latilla and his brother assigned the shares to a special holding company, Kirkland Lake Proprietary Mines. Not much of a gamble, they felt, in winning control of Kirkland Lake's only producing mine.

Already a rough settlement of log cabins called Slabtown huddles near the Tough-Oakes' operation. During late summer evenings miners hewed their family homes where coal oil lamps now light one or two narrow rooms and wood stuffed box stoves throw warmth and cooking heat. Two miles west around the south bay corner of Kirkland Lake's white-capped water, another collection of cabins is tumbling together on the Teck-Hughes' property. Tom Martin first arrived here "just after Christmas of 1911" to build a Stopping Place for prospectors. A year later he and his wife Marie lived there alone and ran the only boarding house this side of Swastika. Now, though, Tom Hough operates a pool room close by, while Wilf Foster and Yacht Campbell have started a general store.

Having worked for Routly and Summers of Haileybury surveying many of the Kirkland Lake claims, twenty-seven year old Ruben Yacht Campbell first saw his opportunity for a supplies business here. Why not chance being in at the start of a mining camp like those who prospered at the beginning of Porcupine? Born at Restoule, southwest of Lake Nipissing, Yacht first worked as a teenager on French River lumber drives, then C.P.R. bridge work until in 1910 he ventured north with Ben Case to the wild call of Porcupine. There they first found work with Laird and Routly surveying South Porcupine townsite. Then as the transit work chained farther on through dozens of mining claims he and Ben learned their surveyor's craft. And surviving the 1911 summer, also a lung-seared respect for forest fires.

Laird & Routly tent office, Porcupine, 1910

Reporting to the Haileybury office last year Yacht Campbell met secretary Maude Cross who had come north to live close by her brother Fred and his grocery store in Cobalt. Now, after their September 17 wedding in Caledonia, Ontario, Maude and Yacht live in a store of their honeymoon own in partnership with Wilf Foster at Kirkland Lake. In place of the summer tent, a high and dry log building now contains the store where Maude and Yacht roost on the second floor. At this end of the Swastika trail, where Walter Little turns his haulage team around, their full barrels, boxes and shelves of groceries and dry goods are a mecca for the hundred or so people scattered through the bush from the Teck-Hughes property to Slabtown. Scattered at their starvation peril, Maude Campbell soon realizes. And her household motto, "No wood, no water, no supper!" sets a winter tone for Kirkland Lake survival.

Although now helped by Captain John Murphy, whose wife may have also brought local luck with the birth of a son on August 6, Harry Oakes himself is still trying to rip gold out of his lakeshore shaft. The Cartwright brothers of Haileybury are having little highgrade luck on Bill Wright's showing. Yet the confident Connell brothers, Art Cockeram and Shirley Cragg have refused Bill Wright's offer of a thousand dollars for the excess water claim he overstaked last year. Bob Jowsey, though, and his Haileybury syndicate would be willing to sell their Kirkland Lake Gold Mines property. And Conrad Wettlaufer, whose foundering Silver Centre mine caused him on August 20 to organize Stephen Orr's property into Orr Gold Mines, might listen to a profitable deal.

Furious, however, is Harry Oakes that Clem Foster has given Englishman Latilla strait-jacket control of the Tough-Oakes. Furthermore, not only did Foster transfer control of Harry's Sylvanite Gold Mines but two months after he returned to Haileybury from England the Tough-Oakes stock, he sold for forty cents a share, is trading on the stock exchange for a dollar. "We have given almost two thirds of the mine away for half its price," Harry accuses, then demands Clem Foster who owns the other third repay the difference. Though Foster had power of attorney, he had no right to sign a final deal without first consulting the other major shareholders, Harry charges. And if Foster does not pay, then Harry swears he will hire lawyer Arthur Slaght of Haileybury to sue. Even though Walter Little has been floating canoe loads of Tough-Oakes' ore across Kirkland Lake all summer and fall, Harry is willing to have his money from the Tough-Oakes' sale tied up in a court case. No one, Harry promises himself, will "swindle" me now or ever out of what is rightfully mine.

The Tough-Oakes operation now hoisting gold ore worth $400 to $600 a ton from the 100 and 200 foot levels. And enough silver is mixed in with this highgrade to pay Walter Little's haulage, the railway shipping and smelter costs. Using mercury amalgamation the five-stamp mill is further treating twelve tons of thirty dollar ore each day. Since the Swastika Mine has closed down, the Tough-Oakes operation remains the only producer in the area; "but now we barely own a share in the mine we prospected and developed," Harry growls; "Never will I lose control of my other Kirkland Lake claims".

And Harry's dream of his own lakeshore mine increasingly haunts him. Even the growth of Swastika station convinces him of future success. While the old waiting room now serves as a telegraph office, the windows of this summer's twenty by thirty foot addition sweat with December steam from more visitors who still believe in gold at Kirkland Lake. Like Porquis Junction's switch into Porcupine, Harry says aloud, Swastika station will someday divert regular trains into the mining field of Kirkland Lake.

If only there was another Noah Timmins who spearheaded Porcupine. Yet other Cobalt mineowners are becoming more and more aware, as their silver reserves are fast depleting, they must soon look for new mineral prospects elsewhere. Still, though, twenty Cobalt mines continue shipping ore. And even though the Drummond family recently sold their Kerr Lake mine, it has been profitably reopened as the Caribou Cobalt. Also with Kerr Lake's water and mud now pumped south into Giroux Lake, Kerr Lake and Crown Reserve miners have found more silver highgrade vein shoots than either company expected. So rich these lake-bed veins are, the Cobalt Lake Mining Company is now seeking permission to pump its own lake dry. In desperate truth, though, the companies must soon admit they are running out of exploration ground.

Meanwhile, lowgrade leftovers of highgrade shoots are also pouring into local mills. Having sold its original mill at the southwest corner of Cobalt Lake to Cobalt Townsite Mine, the Northern Customs Concentrators company is now profitably operating its new eighty-stamp mill at Mileage 104. Nipissing Mine which for so long has mined and milled only highgrade ore now has its own lowgrade mill handling 260 tons a day. In reverse, Buffalo Mine which had first built a lowgrade mill has now added a new highgrade mill to produce silver bullion.

With this year's average price of silver one cent less than last year, mineowners increasingly fret over production costs. And Cobalt town adds to a flesh creeping sense of doom. For the Prospect Hotel, Lowery's store and Bank of Ottawa have burned to the ground, leaving the Hunter Block's west wall singed black. Now besides vagrant boarding houses spread throughout town, only Tom Reilly's North Bay Hotel on Argentite Street and George See's Kenora House on lower Cobalt Street can offer visitors overnight rooms. Though Haileybury and New Liskeard's hotels may be taking most of central Temiskaming's business, the incessant thunder of stamps pounding louder than ever around the Coleman hills reminds everyone that Temiskaming's great wealth was first forged out of the mines of Cobalt. And this 1913 year, their mineral wealth continues to flow— again over thirty million silver ounces.

Joined by Nipissing Central trolley cars Temiskaming's three original towns are almost one. Yet landslides on the leased sections of T.&N.O. track do threaten to sever the thin cord. The last one on November 22 at mileage 111 1/4 tore out tracks and supporting road-bed, interrupting passenger traffic between New Liskeard and Haileybury for several days. T.&N.O. engineers calculate it took ninety-one cars of fill from Cassidy pit to replace the embankment. Another landslide a quarter mile south, on April 16, did not interfere with the trolley run but now motormen constantly eye the track ahead.

NIPISSING CENTRAL RAILWAY CO.

Statement of Wages paid Employees for Year Ended Oct. 31st, 1914.

McDonald, K.	Superintendent	$1,840 00	
Crouch, R. J.	Cashier	1,250 00	
Stewart, W. F.	Land Agent	900 00	
Miller, N. A.	Stenographer	600 00	
Stewart, J.	Janitor	28 00	
Duval, C.	"	32 15	
Lemieux, T.	Motorman	105 49	
Montgomery, A.	Conductor	614 13	
Murray, D. R.	"	878 16	
McAughey, D.	"	1,056 88	
Anderson, G.	"	1,083 09	
Normandy, B.	"	669 37	
McDonald, A. A.	"	982 12	
Curry, F. W.	"	955 60	
Henson, W.	"	346 37	
Quinn, P.	Motorman	1,149 87	
Finlay, F.	"	1,096 17	
Holden, E.	"	986 60	
Carmichael, W.	"	98 17	
Morrell, J. A.	"	1,016 94	
Lyons, H. C.	"	1,012 85	
Parks, W.	"	976 44	
Gangnon, L.	"	74 50	
Faught, T. J.	"	210 62	
McIsaac, N.	Conductor	712 52	
Richardson, R.	"	709 71	
Kilgour, A. H.	"	166 25	
O'Brien, H.	Sanitary Work	3 00	
McMillan, H.	Conductor	180 87	
Presley, W.	"	442 29	
McRae, A. J.	Motorman	661 98	
Fisher, J.	"	280 37	
Garrison, T.	"	512 24	
Moore, N.	"	339 62	
Noble, J.	Conductor	320 36	
Brooks, W.	Motorman	96 37	
Lemieux, P.	"	158 37	
Hoppins, G.	"	43 62	
Stewart, L.	Picketman	4 50	
Draper, J.	Switchman	81 45	
			$22,677 04

Despite its slippery clay foundation Nipissing Central Railway is planning a long life. Surveyors spent the summer plotting an extension from New Liskeard to North Temiskaming. And, in October, Homer Sutcliffe and Ernest Neelands of New Liskeard won contracts to build "a large modern car barn and sub-station" at North Cobalt. The brick and steel, 175 by 64 foot building will house all the company's rolling stock, including two new double-end vestibule cars, each of which has a smoking compartment and seating capacity for fifty people. The larger sub-station connected by a new transmission line to Northern Canada Power Company's sub-station at Cobalt will add another 300 horsepower motor generator to existing power. At a cost of $17,382.20 the car barn will open its doors on December 31; the $1,038.20 sub-station, about January 15, 1914. And by this time the company's snowplow will be out again on the track keeping the line clear for Tri-Town people from Cobalt station to Wabis River bridge.

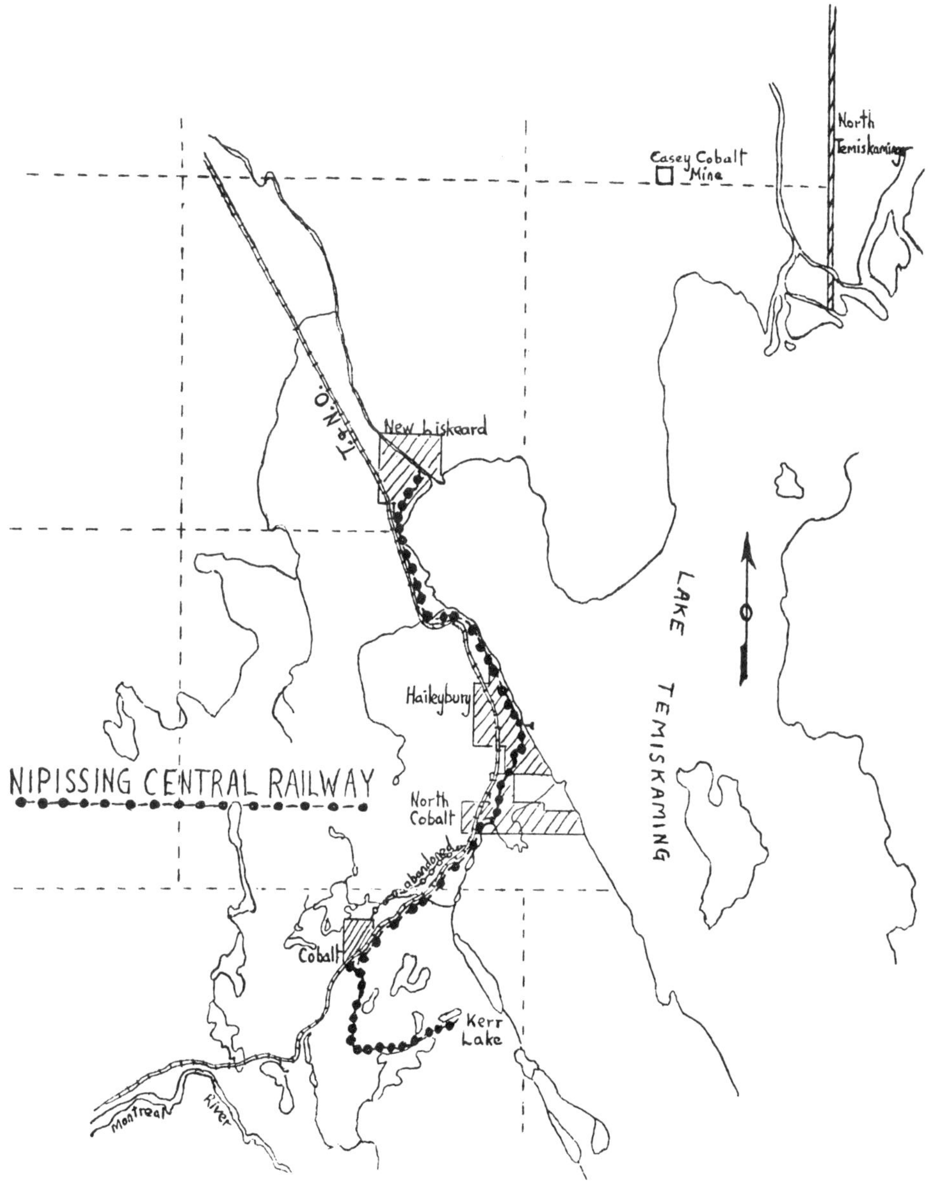
North Temiskaming
Casey Cobalt Mine
T. & N. O.
New Liskeard
LAKE TEMISKAMING
Haileybury
NIPISSING CENTRAL RAILWAY
North Cobalt
abandoned
Cobalt
Kerr Lake
Montreal River

5

The Silence Rose And Became Still

- 1914,1915 -

Since world troubles have stopped silver bullion shipments from London, England, going to the eastern markets of India and China, the price of silver has dropped so low that many of the mines of Cobalt may not afford to stay open. And as their underground workings fill with water, unemployed miners will have to search northwards for work at Porcupine, even Kirkland Lake. Though Cobalt's richer properties continue to produce a total of two and a half tons of pure silver each working day, this January silver price of fifty-seven cents is forcing them to hoard their highgrade until better market days. Yet choosing not to wait, Nipissing Mine on February 14 ships thirty-eight bars containing 453,213 silver ounces. The company almost cancelled delivery, though, after it learned the sales value had fallen to $260,681.16.

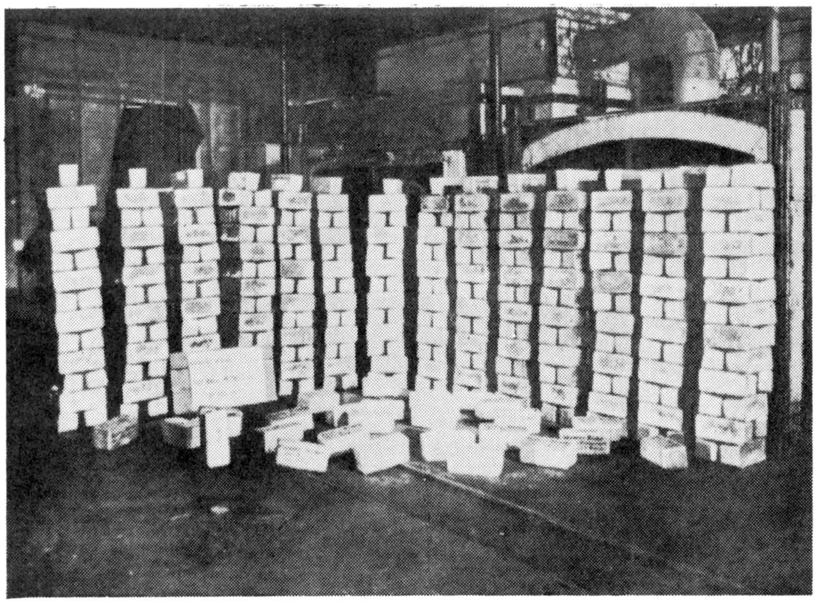

Nipissing Mine silver bullion shipment, February, 1914

Despite the silver slump, the business pulse of past mining production years still beats strongly in Cobalt. Out of charred ground where the Cobalt Hotel once stood rises the silver town's new town hall. Like the Royal Exchange this large building on Presley Street boasts fireproof brick construction. By July, town clerk Robert O'Gorman promises, municipal offices, police court and council chambers will cover the main floor. Police chief Norman Burke with constables Sharp and Newton might even have an office here. The spacious assembly hall on the second floor has enough room for any kind of town meeting. Just as much space as the farmer's market in the basement.

Almost within touching distance immediately west remains the former town hall facing Silver Street. With their wholesale store clinging to the south side of this soon-to-be-abandoned building, Charles Reckin and Son wonder who will buy its elegant three storeys. The fire bell still hangs from its belfry and the tall walls of moulded metal flash in the sun. Especially on blue-shadowed summer afternoons, the *Cobalt Nugget* and George Taylor Hardware staffs remember from across Silver Street. Just south of the Grand Theatre and *Nugget* office, past the Y.M.C.A., where recreation secretary George Modler is trying to keep the pool water warm enough for winter swimming, and around the Mines Hospital corner will stand a new nurses' residence on Grandview Avenue. Not a fireproof building, however, one of the main reasons the new town hall example is being built. But regardless, filled with the energy of their lifeblood mines, Cobalters cannot slow down long enough to worry about tomorrow.

Just as stubborn is Harry Oakes at Kirkland Lake where in February he incorporates his four lakeside claims as Lake Shore Mines. Since litigation against Clem Foster has frozen his share of any profits from the Tough-Oakes' property, he is sure public shares of half his Lake Shore stock will raise sufficient money for exploring farther north out under the lake. Out into the main ore break, he explains again— to anyone willing to listen. Wording the company prospectus, lawyer Arthur Slaght describes Harry, Ernie Martin, Bill Wright and mine manager John Morrison as loyal directors. Dividing half the two million shares among his family supporters and himself, Harry expects he can sell some 150,000 of the remaining shares for immediate cash. Yet even at twenty-five cents a share, locals warn him few people will gamble on his "hair-brained" belief in golden treasure under the lake. Previously refused a $10,000 loan from George Bagshaw's Union Bank in Haileybury, he has vowed vengeance. And when Jimmy Doig stopped Harry's credit for supplies from his Swastika general store, Harry's bitterness grew. Now, though, he can gloat since Arthur Slaght has persuaded Temiskaming's M.L.A. Robert Shillington to exert his Conservative Party influence in establishing a Federal post office at Kirkland Lake. Then appointed postmaster on February 16, Wilf Foster takes all Kirkland Lake business away from Doig's Swastika office. And forget about buying anything at Doig's store, Harry orders his miners. And forget the stingy

Union Bank. Ever since Allan Kirkpatrick, manager of the Royal Bank in Haileybury, advanced him a small loan, Harry has sworn to boycott the Union Bank forever.

Tough-Oakes bunkhouse

Maybe Harry Oakes would be less angry if he could still curl away his frustrations in Haileybury. Especially in the town's current competition for the Englehart Cup: fifteen end games can weaken anyone's rigid temper. Starting Saturday evening, February 14, New Liskeard's challenge of Haileybury's present hold on the trophy alternates for three weeks between the towns' clubhouses.

First matches at Haileybury, February 14:

	Haileybury		New Liskeard	Haileybury		New Liskeard
Skip	J. Rankin		S. Ritchie	R. Budd		A. Stephenson
Vice	C. Lindberg	v	M. McLeod	H. Dunbar	v	Dr. Summers
Second	A. Forrest		F. Francis	F. Day		F. Binkley
Lead	I. Solomon		E. Hansman	J. McCuaig		P. Graham
Score:	14	-	7	11		19

New Liskeard wins on total points

Second matches at New Liskeard, February 21:

	Haileybury		New Liskeard	Haileybury		New Liskeard
Skip	J. Rankin		S. Ritchie	W. Gordon		A. Stephenson
Vice	C. Lindberg	v	C. Alton	R. Budd	v	Dr. Summers
Second	A. Forrest		F. Haynes	F. Day		T. Magladery
Lead	I. Solomon		W. Armstrong	J. McCuaig		F. Binkley
Score:	18	-	13	15		19

Haileybury wins on total points

Third matches at Haileybury, February 28:

	Haileybury		New Liskeard	Haileybury		New Liskeard
Skip	C. Lindberg		H. Brown	H. Dunbar		W. Evans
Vice	J. Rankin	v	M. McLeod	R. Budd	v	F. Hutchinson
Second	A. Forrest		C. Walkinshaw	S. Forneri		C. Alton
Lead	I. Solomon		P. Graham	F. Shillington		W. Armstrong
Score:	17	-	10	6	-	17

New Liskeard wins on total points wins the series and the Englehart Cup

Winning agrees with business life in New Liskeard. During the final week in February Messrs Sproule and Soucie swing wide the Armstrong Street door of "The Man's Store" in Yates' building across from Magladery's Hardware. And a week later excited news sweeps through town when the March 6 issue of the *New Liskeard Speaker* reports Temiskaming and Hudson Bay Mining Company's discovery of a rich gold vein at Porcupine's Dome Lake Mining and Milling property. Will the New Liskeard mining company, the first publicly organized company to hold mineral ground at Cobalt, repeat its famous dividend success? The town's loyal shareholders want to know. Having acquired control last November of this Dome Lake Property on part of lot six, concession one of Tisdale township, George Taylor, Angus McKelvie and company directors had advised manager A.H. Brown to continue drifting from the deepest of the mine's four shafts. This Tuesday afternoon after blasting a drift round on the 115 foot level, miners found the one inch wide vein heavy with free gold. Maybe this showing will lead into another bonanza like that of neighbouring Dome Mine. And maybe the idle ten-stamp mill can start crushing additional low grade ore which is bound to follow.

As if to celebrate New Liskeard's good fortune Tom Magladery, on Wednesday, March 18, invites all local customers to his annual delivery of Massey Harris farm machinery, "Be at the warehouse early to avoid confusion, between 10:00 a.m. and noon." After a sit-down dinner the guests can then shift to the Opera House for an afternoon moving picture show followed by a dramatic performance of "The Fortune Hunters". Watching the morning parade of harnessed horses tugging farm equipment over the snow packed ruts of Whitewood Avenue reminds New Liskeard its greatest summer fortune may best be found in ploughing clay lands north rather than mining any underlying Precambrian rocks.

Springtime mud, Whitewood Avenue, New Liskeard

Latchford, though, wishes it even had a choice. Having lost its Montreal River shipping business to the T.&N.O.'s Elk Lake line, Latchford's prospects continue to shrink. And now that the Empire Lumber Company, whose Montreal River sawmill has not trimmed a stick of wood in the last three years, is moving its planing equipment south, the village's future looks bleakest. Yet only five years ago its residents talked of their town's growing stature. At that time, one of the T.&N.O.'s main reasons for laying the spur line to Haileybury wharf was so Empire Lumber could build a jackladder and load logs on to flat cars for delivery to its Latchford mill. But two months ago, on February 9, Empire Lumber Company president Charles Warren cancelled the agreement and surrendered ownership of the Haileybury jackladder to the T.&N.O. Commission.

Owning much of the mineral ground at Cobalt the T.&N.O. Commission is also busy rearranging mining leases there. Since the new English syndicate has merged control of its City of Cobalt property with his Cobalt Lake property to form the Mining Corporation of Canada, Sir Henry Pellatt as Canadian president is now applying to have many of the old-time leases assigned to his newest company. On March 23 the Commissioners agreed to reassign Townsite Extension Mines' Cobalt station grounds lease. On April 15 they further reassign the Cobalt Townsite and City of Cobalt Mining Company leases. Adding these lands to his Cobalt Lake property, which he finally has permission to drain, and his Little Nipissing Mine, Pellatt can now thoroughly explore the remaining untouched rocks under Cobalt town and lake. And with Townsite Mine having previously bought Northern Customs Concentrators, he has a second mill to treat an expected overflow of silver ore. Matt Fairlie, who stayed as manager of Northern Customs the Townsite company has since renamed Cobalt Reduction Company, will stay on again as general manager of Mining Corporation's total mine-mill operation.

City of Cobalt Mine (Mining Corporation), McKinley-Darragh mill in left background, Cobalt

Townsite Mine, Mining Corporation, Cobalt

Less satisfactory has been the reappointment of Albert Freeman as president of McIntyre Mines at Timmins. John Bickell, who has learned the honest dealing of finances through his Trethewey Mine at Cobalt, is furious. How could McIntyre shareholders favour Freeman's return after his jail term for fraud? Furthermore, he says, how can this bamboozler help rescue a mine unable to find paying gold ore? Since mine manager Dick Ennis has said assay values are increasing with the shaft down to 300 feet, Bickell suspects Freeman has returned in hopes of picking the company's pocket. And what then if miners do break into gold shoots as finger tempting as the fabulous wealth glittering in Hollinger's underground stopes?

In the middle of Temiskaming's wealth New Liskeard has found an inexpensive way to cheer itself through the long winter into spring. On April 17 the *Speaker* writes of last week's bowling prize won by Charlie Wilder with a high score of 254. And the Bankers defeated the Hardware men in the first game of a local series, 2,438 to 2,141 pins. So far this week with one game score of 211, W. Wonch is league leader. Next week New Liskeard's three teams will enter the Haileybury tournament against Ike Solomon's Trundlers and Harry Browning's King Pins. Last year's unbeatable team, The Champions of Jay Perrault, W. Froggett, Sam Ritchie, Cutt Woodward and Jake Solomon along with the "Isch-Ka-Bibbles" of C. Wilder, E. Lapointe, P. Bassett, R. McLeod, O. Solomon and The Grand Unions of Bucher, McMahon, Cattley, Grills, Rennels are certain they will bring trophies back to New Liskeard.

None of their bowling scores C.C. Farr will report as editor of the *Haileyburian*, however, for on May 1 he retires. And his newspaper becomes the property of the Haileyburian Printing Company. Carl Green who first worked in *New Liskeard Speaker's* mechanical department before becoming a reporter with the *Cobalt Nugget* is taking control. Suffering from throat cancer C.C. spends May month pulling himself away from the ink stained desk and on June 11 blots his last article, a memorial tribute to Elizabeth Elston. His chosen words reveal as much about C.C. Farr as they do the deceased:

After an illness extending over the past month during which time little hope was held out for her recovery on account of advanced age, Mrs. J.P. Elston died at her home on Amwell Street on Tuesday morning. She was born in Devonshire, England 80 years ago last September. With her husband she came to Canada some 45 years ago settling first in Montreal and latterly in East Bolton, Que. where they resided until 10 years ago. At that time Mr. and Mrs. Elston moved to Haileybury where they have lived retired ever since.

Had Mrs. Elston lived until Saturday of this week she would have been able, with her husband to celebrate their golden wedding. She was married on June 13th, just fifty years ago.

Two children survive, Mrs. S. Atkinson and Mrs. (Dr.) H.R. Codd, both of whom reside in Haileybury. The funeral took place on Wednesday morning to St. Paul's Church and interment was made in the Haileybury cemetery.

It is seldom that a funeral in Haileybury has attracted more attention than that of the late dear old Lady, Mrs. Elston. She won her way to all our hearts, simply through her own personality. We just loved her for herself, and who could help it. She was the personification of a kind heart, a nature bubbling over with the humanities, and one that was never tired of doing good works, unobtrusively. Beside all this, she had a cheeriness of disposition that was fairly infectious, an innate optimism that has brought comfort to many an affliction. And at the back of that, there was the most wonderful spirit of quiet organization. She, when she realized the inevitable "fiat", straightway started "to put her house in order." I happened to have been chosen by her as pall bearer. When we, those who had been thus honoured, compared notes, we found that she herself had made the selection of us all, and we all understood the tie that had bound. During that simple but impressive ceremony, by which the English Church bury its dead I looked around, and I found with me, in that sacred Edifice, men and women of all denominations, gathered together to do the last honours to one so universally beloved and respected. I have nothing to say regarding the details, for they will be described by others. All I want to do is to pay due tribute to the memory of one whom I loved and admired, and to express my sympathy to her bereaved husband, and children.

Appointed Lay Reader and Catechist on January 20, James White, in surplice and cassock, leads Rev. John Popey's funeral procession south on Meridian Avenue, through Lawlortown down Elliot Street to LakeShore Road, south again along the old colonization road dipping down by the brickyard, over the short timbered bridge beside the boulder beach and up the slope into a tunnel of poplar trees, until turning right off Mill Creek road up through the cemetery gate. Up to where Elizabeth Elston who first came from

Liskeard in Cornwall will be laid to final rest only five miles away from the namesake Canadian town. While James White lifted aloft the altar cross, the Elstons donated to their Haileybury church, Rev. Popey's last words of burial rise above the blow of breeze off blue Temiskaming's shore.

The same breeze has blown shivers across the waters of Kirkland Lake. Two weeks ago, in the early morning darkness of May 29, Henry Cecil's four English engineers carrying their detailed geological reports and Burnside diamond drill core were drowned when the *Empress of Ireland* they had boarded at Quebec City only hours before collided with a collier, exploded and sank in the Strait of Belle Isle. Now without solid mineral evidence from the engineers, H.G. Latilla in London, England, dares not risk optioning any other expensive part of the Kirkland Lake area. Leaving it to an early death? Who else has the development money to spend?

Regardless Temiskaming life must turn to the coming provincial election. And on Monday, June 22, the political leaders of Cobalt, Haileybury and New Liskeard travel to Englehart's Orange Hall to nominate their candidates. By 2:00 p.m. the returning officer, Dr. T. Stoddard of Cobalt, declares Tom Magladery, Conservative; Arthur Roebuck, Liberal; T.G. Mills, Socialist. Noisiest foot stomping sounds for Magladery.

Hearing of the results, Bob Jenkins remembers 1906 when he and Art Geeling had sold their Firstbrook mining claim to John Lumsden, then paid $100 for a sailboat from Hamilton and named it *Flirt*. Five feet wide and twenty-five feet long with a stabilizing centre board they used it for prospecting the rocky shoreline of Lake Temiskaming. But most enjoyably they entered the holiday races. And everytime *Flirt's* 400 square feet of silk sails, with spinnaker and balloon jib, filled with wind they defeated their main opponent Arthur Roebuck "who hated losing".

If the political candidates cannot visit every township in Temiskaming, at least the different telephone companys might carry their messages. On June 30, F.J. Armstrong and Silvanus Trevail's Kerns township Highland Telephone Company signs a T.&N.O. agreement permitting the exchange of local and long distance calls through Uno Park railway station. So now the ninety Kerns farmers with house phones can talk to a larger world. With Cochrane's new railway station having opened on January 21, so too has the T.&N.O. connected with Cochrane Telephone Company. Just as it has with Porcupine Telephone Company at South Porcupine.

How much longer before Temiskaming's telephone systems become one? For on January 31, Alfred Reese sold all the phones, boards and poles of his Elk Lake Telegraph and Telephone Company to the T.&N.O. Commission for $4,650. Even the phone line to Gowganda, the T.&.N.O. now possesses. Yet the shareholders of New Liskeard's Temiscaming Telephone Company, proud of its title as the northern district's largest independent telephone company, are preparing rival expansion plans of their own.

Elk Lake, new government bridge to west shore

Elk Lake, King George Hotel, Main Street

Having left their bachelor cabin and telephone at Gowganda to represent the Rideau Aquatic Club in Ottawa, prospectors Fred Thompson and Bob Gamble have won June's annual 200 mile canoe race from Mont Laurier to Ste. Rose, Quebec— in a record forty-eight hours. Tirelessly paddling stiff-armed these bush-hardened partners even shot the Long Sault rapids near Grenville— something local Indians had never dared to do. Just another summer trip, Fred and Bob say of their amazing feat. Then they return north in perennial search of minerals. Into the bush where telephones never ring.

On July 1, at its park out the North Road, New Liskeard's Athletic Association stages Dominion day games and races. Yet since Tom Magladery won the provincial election two days ago with an overwhelming majority of 500 votes, New Liskeard is already in a festive mood. Not Arthur Roebuck, however, who defeated a second time chose not to join Magladery's victory parade or risk catcalls in the Opera House's sweltering heat that evening.

So hot and dry is today's south Temiskaming weather the *Speaker* comments on the "Gloomy prospect" for farmers. Though pastures remain green, the lack of rain since spring-time threatens crop failures; "Never before in the history of Temiskaming did the prospect of the farmer have so sombre an appearance."

But withering weather only helps Haileybury celebrate its Old Boys' Reunion, during the week of July 13. Banners and flags drape downtown streets while horse races and baseball games out the West Road at Farr's Park, boat races on Lake Temiskaming, and football at North Cobalt distract visitors tired of talking over old times. Not too many people tire, though. And their handshaking cheers muffle the clang of picks and shovels levelling crushed mine rock dumped along both sides of the trolley line south of Main Street. North of the Vendome Hotel, Nipissing Central trackmen are still prying rails up to the height of LakeShore Road's freshly gravelled surface. By summer's end ninety-four carloads of fill should prevent mud from oozing upwards again. And 170 carloads are covering the longer stretch of New Liskeard's LakeShore Road.

After one slow run through Haileybury this crowded reunion week all the uniformed N.C.R. conductors know they cannot escape town without some reveller pulling out their shirttails. Having to stamp the trolley's danger-warning pedal bell all the way along Ferguson Avenue is like inviting pranksters aboard for another try.

Haileybury race track, West Road, Farr's new house upper left

Meanwhile Benny Hollinger, Alec Gillies, George Bannerman, Sandy McIntyre, Jack Miller, Tom Middleton and Clary Dixon reminisce over their Porcupine discoveries five years ago. Noah Timmins, brother Henry and the rest of their original LaRose Syndicate, the McMartin brothers and David Dunlap, have entertainment suites at the Matabanick. Jack Hammell, Jack Munroe, Tommy Saville and Leo Erenhous recall Elk Lake's earliest times. Bob Jowsey, James Wood, Charlie Keeley, Absalom Gibson, Ben Killoran, Stod Forneri, Mark Harris, Monty Montgomery, H. Armour Smith, Conrad

Wettlaufer, Cyril Young toast their Silver Centre luck. Bill Adair, Ed deCamps, Nat and Neil Oslund, Pete McGinley, Walter Penley all prospected there but missed out on the best ground.

Clem Foster opens his Main Street house to the mining crowd of Cobalt. At his LakeShore Road house Arthur Ferland reminds Tom Gibson, then minister of mines, of the farm acreage claims he, Bill Chambers and the Russel brothers first staked and how Professor Miller praised the Little Vein before the Nipissing crowd from New York bought it all. Except for the ground under Peterson Lake which everyone forgot. Next north of Ferland's Florence Street corner, the Cartwrights invite all their Temiskaming Mine friends, Charlie Richardson talks of the original silver discovery, Norman Fisher of management problems.

At his house on Rorke Avenue, between Amwell and Marcella streets, Colonel Hay parties with William Trethewey, John Bickell, Alex Longwell, Colonel Leonard, Milton Hersey, Charlie Denison. Out of Trethewey's 1904 curiosity emerged his own mine, then the Coniagas and the Buffalo.

From New Liskeard George Taylor, Tom McCamus and Angus McKelvie come to talk of their legendary Temiskaming and Hudson Bay Mining Company success. Frank Culver and Alfred Young thank them for selling the Silver Queen which lead on to fortune at Beaver Mine. Kalil Farah returns to recall the early days of his Big Pete Canadian Mine and Cobalt Central. Murdy McLeod still marvels at his early success while surveying with George Glendinning of New Liskeard.

On Brewster Street, John Black exchanges stories about his missed McKinley-Darragh option opportunity, the Finucanes certainly enjoyed instead. And his Nancy-Helen property never did measure up to hopes. On Georgina Avenue, Bob Shillington talks of his arrival in Cobalt with Heman H. Lang and Bill Powell of Ottawa to lease the City of Cobalt properties. Downtown in his Main Street pool room, Ned Wright entertains with rugged memories of his brother Marty's Kerr Lake discoveries. So many prospectors, those who made money and those who almost did, stop to greet one another at the Main Street-Ferguson Avenue intersection that the swinging door into the Maple Leaf bar room falls off its hinges. Remember the bush trails, the portages, the blood-thirsty flies, the thrill of diabase and a calcite vein? How many claims has George Smith's office recorded since 1905? How many maps has Cyril Knight drawn of Temiskaming ground? Who last told of how Dr. W.G. Miller had dreamed up Cobalt's name?

Out of all the tales of prospecting days stirs a deep feeling for earliest pioneer times; for the Farrs, the Cobbolds, the Johnsons, the Girouxs, Westrons, Blackwalls, Norfolks, Oslunds, Atkinsons, Bridens, Codds, Hennessys, Murphys, Adairs, Flemings, Berrys, Robbs, McQuarries, Littles, Elliotts and all the others who came to Haileybury before Cobalt's discovery, before the railway. Easy it is to forget names in today's blur of faces filling the town's Old Boys' Reunion streets, hotels and dance floors.

Haileybury Old Boys Reunion, July 13 - 18, 1914
Looking towards Main Street corner - Maple Leaf Hotel

Too young is Kirkland Lake to have memories. But Bill Wright and Ed Hargreaves can count themselves residents of Haileybury. Jack "Shorty" Stirrup works in George Jamieson's billiards academy across Browning Street from the Vendome Hotel. Dr. Robins still pulls teeth. Dave Elliott lives on Marcella Street, John Reamsbottom on Meridian Avenue. Harry Oakes stays at John Weedon's boarding house on Browning Street whenever he delivers another sample next door for Davey John to assay. The Hughes brothers, Jack Matchett, John Hunton, Stephen Orr, Fred Bidgood, Joe Grozelle, Arthur Cockeram, Shirley Cragg live here. Fred Connell keeps a room at the Vendome Hotel. While Haileybury lawyers Ed Kearney, Fred Day and Wes Gordon, Arthur Slaght and his brother Hugh are always ready to organize their companies.

What better way to end Haileybury's Reunion than the formal opening of Temiskaming's District Court House! While the Friday afternoon sun glares down on a platform stage facing the shirt-sleeved crowd in front of the court house, Ontario's Premier W.H. Hearst praises the district's growing greatness. Mining Recorder George T. Smith speaking for the Old Boys and Haileybury, as the "gateway to the clay belt", says the "government has made no mistake choosing Haileybury for the district Seat." Mr. Barton of Cobalt adds his agreement. Newly elected M.P.P. Tom Magladery grins that Haileybury is welcome to its gateway claim, but New Liskeard is "gateway to the world." After ten speakers have exhausted themselves, Haileybury Mayor Neil McAulay, for the sake of those people who have questioned holding this ceremony before the court house is complete, explains the premature date was chosen to coincide with Reunion Week. And even though Ed Hargreaves' painters have not yet started the outside trim nor inside rooms, no one should forget this colourful day.

Even though the lady high diver who frightened everyone at Farr's Park with her leap into a puddle of water finally misses the raised canvas sheet in another show next week at North Bay, young Leslie McFarlane, one of the public school principal's sons, would never forget the parachute freedom of these dandelion-blown summer days. He would remember "invading Ferland's lots beyond the new high school to pick wild roses" and farther north "to Foster's Field for wild strawberries." Especially sweet was the fruit in among the rotting foundation of Heard's original log farm house and barn perched on the south bank of the stream which cut the field's northern edge. Temiskaming Heights, Clem Foster named this subdivision property after he bought the farm; but no one ever built, except for his own small hunting lodge at the northeast corner, a hundred yards up the slope from Latchford Street. Raspberries from Ferland's lots overflowed lard pails in July. And all day wagon journeys to blueberry stained rocks at Fleming's Corner or smoother *Meteor* rides to Martineau and Paradis bays filled August washtubs to the brim.

George T. and Rosemary Smith

Haileybury Old Home Week, July 13 - 18, 1914
Looking south along Ferguson Avenue from Browning Street corner

City of Haileybury, steamship

Leslie McFarlane would remember his companions who skipped summer streets around his Marcella home: "Cyril and Ted Atkinson and Thyra, Roy O'Neil and Tom and Mary O'Gorman, Cora and Wilbur Scharfe, Willie Durrell and Andy Farrell, Tim McDonough, Jane and Margaret and Helen Caldbick and Joe and Sam, the Brownlee girls, Bill McCagherty." And there would always be the lake. "On lazy summer days you watched the *Lady Minto* or the *[Lady] Alexandria* inching their way southward with the log booms from the Head, and you counting the seconds elapsing between the white plume of steam and the distant sound of the saluting whistle."

Meteor with picnickers at Montreal River landing

Piled on the foredeck of each tug boat were birch logs ready to drop down the stoke hole to fire twin boilers below. Cyril Atkinson would remember he and brother Ted riding the smaller service tug *Alert* with friend John Gillies out to these company boats. From the piston rods of the twin-cylinder engine placed in the steel hull stern "great cranks twenty to thirty feet long came up to the crank shaft joining the paddle wheels."

From the shore it was quite a sight to see these big tug boats towing the immense booms of logs down the lake. The booms must have been a mile or more long and, in spite of the power of the boats, they moved very slowly. Often you would see them early in the morning off Chief's Island and by night-fall you would see them just below Farr's Island.

Scorning Bill Ferris' boat house near the Haileybury market building where parents could rent canoes, rowboats or launches, swim-suited boys paddled their log rafts through summer heat. They glanced up Amwell Street to the Plaza Theatre and the skating rink stretched behind and remembered the player-organ's two tunes from winter. Around the warmth of the pot-bellied stove young skaters had traded cigarette cards with coloured pictures of professional hockey players, then gazed at the dressing room walls where autographed names of Cyclone Taylor, Duke Keats, Paddy Moran, the goalie, and Horace Gaul were fading away. Boot laced tight they had sliced their own marks over the wooden floor, 300 pound goalie Billy Nicholson also carved three years before, to watch Tom Montgomery waltz his gliding daughters to an icy *Swan Lake* sleep. What of the big box sleigh rides from Dunseath's or McCleary's livery stables? Or bob-sledding down Browning Street, all the way from the railway station past the pump house out on to the lake? Or snowshoe parties? Or the Christmas tree hunt? Yet none of this could compare to the bare-legged, wind drifting, cloud-staring days of summer.

But to a cooling end, Leslie McFarlane knew, they would come in September when school began. And this 1914 year his entrance into high school would start a new adventure. Principal Wilson in his grey top hat, morning coat, four-in-hand tie and white spats who "will not even allow brother and sister to walk home together" rules the strict academic world above; while "Porkie" Flynn and George Cole drill their mining class in the basement below. But who could ever match Leslie McFarlane's swooping public school nemesis, the apron-waisted, ruler-wielding Sarah Flegg?

In the swamp strewn bush of Teck township no child nor adult dares offer their naked legs to the bloodthirsty flies. Too harsh a playground is Kirkland Lake camp for carefree children, yet not much longer if the other companies there can start finding rich gold like the Tough-Oakes'. And since April when the twenty-six mile transmission line from Charlton's hydro plant was completed, Kirkland Lake mines have the electrical power to drive hard working machines, even brighten small cabin light bulbs.

Haileybury Public School Entrance Class, 1914

Front row from left are: Russell Whitely, M.J. Hennessy, Leslie McFarlane, George Morden, Bramwell Watkins, Brian Caldwell, Tom Sharp, Cyril Atkinson, Enuch Nelson and Jack Lamb.
Second row from left: Frances Ebbit, Alice Johnston, Jane Caldbick, Olea Montgomery, Cynthia Faulkner, John MacArthur, Andy Farrell, Bill Steel and Jack Dunn.
Third Row from left: Ollie Thompson, Annie Newlands and Minerva Reid.

Already wood-fired smoke has stopped belching from Kirkland Lake's Tough-Oakes' steam plant and Lake Shore Mine is installing an electrically driven six drill compressor and hoist.

Encouraged by Charlton's cheaper power, even Cobalt's prosperous, cost-conscious Nipissing Mining Company has agreed to take a chance option on Kirkland Lake's Teck-Hughes' property. Alarmed by the barren rock it has hosed clean along the east side of Cobalt Lake, Nipissing must find fresh mineral ground for future business.

Charlton hydro electric power plant

Louis Roberge and Arthur Galoska have also begun fidgetting over their Cobalt futures. Beginning work four years ago in Bob Lowery's tobacco and confectionery store at Cobalt, Louis quit after the Prospect Avenue store burned down last year to start his own at Swastika. This summer he has moved it to the Slabtown site next to Tough-Oakes Mine. So has Arthur Galoska moved his hardware business from Presley Street in Cobalt. Burned out by the Cobalt Hotel-Opera House fire of two years ago, he too started a new business at Swastika but now believes in a better future at Kirkland Lake. But not Jack Matchett, now Swastika's harness and shoemaker. Having seen his village's two gold mines close last year he so distrusts any future he has sold his Kirkland Lake claim, immediately south of Bill Wright's original discovery, to Harry Oakes, Dan Murray and Swastika storeowner brothers Andrew and Frank Duncan. Also unsettled is Dr. Dorsey who as assistant to Dr. Fisher of New Liskeard had provided medical aid to the T.&N.O. construction workers on the Porcupine-Iroquois Falls branch line in 1911, then married the New Liskeard office nurse Miss Reed and two years ago started a home and new medical practice in Swastika. This summer, though, rather than follow the trail to Kirkland Lake he has decided to sell his practice to Dr. J.D. Wilson and go to the busier location of Iroquois Falls where the T.&N.O. on May 23 opened a passenger station to serve the new plant of Abitibi Power and Paper Company.

Dr. Dorsey and his wife spurn the established ways of New Liskeard where on August 2 the Agricultural Society holds its annual field day. Better are pioneer beginnings, the couple believe, but not quite to the remote extreme of Kirkland Lake. Then on August 4 they wonder if all peaceful moves may not be in vain as Great Britain declares war on Germany.

Yesterday, Kaiser Wilhelm's troops invaded Belgium; to honour its Belgian, French, Russian, Serbian allies, the British Empire now chooses to fight Germany and Austro-Hungary. What arrogant madness motivates Germany—against the might of the British Empire, surely any battle will be short?

Not short enough, however, to rescue today's falling sales of silver. And from the fourth to the seventh day of August the London silver market remains closed. When it does open, Cobalt's mineowners must face heavier costs of insuring their shipments of bullion to London.

Who in Temiskaming can identify with military quarrels across the ocean? Especially those people in the southern half of the district who now live in daily fear of losing their hometown jobs. With more silver mines closing, Tom Magladery, M.P.P., leads an August 18 delegation of New Liskeard, Haileybury and Cobalt mayors and Chamber of Commerce presidents to Queen's Park asking for more public works in Temiskaming. The fifty-three cent price of silver has forced so many mines to close, miners are begging for work. And the falling demand for lumber is depriving them, as well as regular loggers, of any chance for sawmill or bush work this winter. Temiskaming farmers are hiring a few men to clear land but the wage of eighteen dollars a month with board is "pretty low". Help New Ontario, Magladery's delegation pleads, by building a Nipissing Central Railway extension to North Temiskaming. And so stimulate construction jobs and northern agriculture. Any further delay of this N.C.R. line could mean the Canadian Pacific company which talks of extending its rail line up the east side of Lake Temiskaming to Ville Marie and possibly beyond to the Head of the Lake would steal business from Ontario. Further help the north by pushing the T.&N.O. branch line from Elk Lake into Gowganda. Stimulate more construction jobs and more mining. Without government assistance to carry the Tri-Town area over these depressed mining and lumbering times, many local industries will also fail. Take, for example, Tom Magladery says, the plight of Kalil Farah's New Liskeard Brick Company. It was started by hand in 1897 by Mr. Scott who eventually bought machinery to press bricks as town demand grew, then sold the operation to the Brick Company which borrowed money until it transferred control to Pete Farah who now because of Temiskaming's present slump in building construction must close the plant. If Kalil cannot afford to keep a business going, how many others can? And how many more men of Temiskaming will be put out of work?

Firemen's reception, New Liskeard, August 18, 1914

Depressed by poor lumber sales and frustrated by continued delays in completing the T.&N.O. spur as far as his Haileybury mill yard, Clem Foster sells the idle property to the Riordon Pulp and Paper Company which will convert it to a rossing plant. Unlike Haileybury, some of whose LakeShore Road residents still legally resist having freight trains interrupt their scenic view, New Liskeard can rejoice this August month as its T.&N.O. spur line is finally completed. South of Bishop Latulipe's New Liskeard Palace, the tracks cross LakeShore Road bending northeast to the wharf. Yet because of repairs to the opened control dam at the foot of Lake Temiskaming the water is too low for boats to dock and the new eight car siding which stretches to the south end of Armstrong Street stands empty.

New Liskeard harbour and dock

Not all of the T.&N.O.'s summer work has been stalled or left useless, though. After electrifying its branch line from Cobalt station to Kerr Lake Junction, the Commission has given it to Nipissing Central. Running over the track along the east side of the station grounds, trolley cars bound for Kerr Lake will not interfere with the main T.&N.O. trains. And with more electricity now being consumed, the Northern Ontario Light and Power Company is employing more men to install equipment for harnessing 4,000 more horsepower at Fountain Falls on the Montreal River, 10 3/4 miles below Gillies Depot. Besides a siding for Northern Customs' new eighty-stamp mill at Mileage 104, the Commission has just built another 514 foot one for six cars at the north end of its Cobalt yard. And it has almost finished grading thirty-one cars of gravel for a wagon roadway to this Dynamite Delivery siding. Thankful are the people of Cobalt that boxes of explosives will no longer pile dangerously high beside the station house where accident or arson always threatened to blast a crater out of the town's central Square. "Safety first" repeats the Commission which this 1914 year has "inaugurated the first All Steel Passenger Trains in Canada." Since 1905 T.&N.O. trains have carried almost five million passengers "and not killed or seriously injured one."

Despite the despairingly lower forty-six cent price of silver, people still shop Cobalt's street. Smaller mines are closing but the giants of LaRose, Nipissing, Mining Corporation, Coniagas, Kerr Lake, Crown Reserve, McKinley-Darragh-Savage mines are still producing millions of ounces. How much longer, though, before Cobalt town finds its streets left lonely, like scratch marks across the thin skulls of emptied mine caverns? Yet, for now, the search for cheaply mined silver governs all. At the northwest Prospect Avenue-Silver Street corner, Coniagas Mine is collaring a shaft. And to save its neighbouring store from being crushed under dumped rock, Jamieson's Meat Market on Silver Street either has to move off the Coniagas land or pay for a trestle to tram the rock elsewhere. Cheering their handsteeling and mucking heroes at West Cobalt Park, Labour Day spectators know what is most important in Cobalt.

Northern Customs Concentrators, Mileage 104 mill

Cobalt Square

After losing two provincial elections in Temiskaming, Arthur Roebuck has finally decided what comes first in his life. He is selling the *Herald's* flatbed press to his journeyman printer, Ernest Hand, and leaving New Liskeard to resume his study of law in Toronto. Having stopped this study more than ten years ago to help his publisher brother, he now leaves *The Herald* newspaper and his own *Cobalt Citizen* creation to find victory elsewhere.

Draining Cobalt Lake - 1914

Silver Mining Companies, 1914

Name of Company or Owner.	Name of Mine.	Locality.	P. O. Address of Manager, etc.
Aladdin Cobalt Company, Limited	Silver Queen	Cobalt	Cobalt.
Associated Gold Mines of Western Australia Limited, The	Keeley	South-Lorrain Tp.	Silver Centre.
Bailey Cobalt Mines, Limited	Bailey	Cobalt	Giroux Lake.
Beaver Consolidated Mines, Limited	Beaver	Cobalt	Cobalt.
Buffalo Mines, Limited, The	Buffalo	Cobalt	Cobalt.
Cart Lake Cobalt-Silver Mines, Limited	Peterson Lake	Cobalt	Cobalt.
Casey Cobalt Silver Mining Company, Limited	Casey-Cobalt	Casey Township	New Liskeard.
Chambers-Ferland Mining Company, Limited	Chambers-Ferland	Cobalt	Cobalt.
*City of Cobalt Mining Company, Limited	City of Cobalt	Cobalt	Cobalt.
*Cobalt Townsite Mining Company, Limited	Cobalt Townsite	Cobalt	Cobalt.
Cobalt Comet Mines, Limited	Drummond	Cobalt	Giroux Lake.
*Cobalt Lake Mining Company, Limited	Cobalt Lake	Cobalt	Cobalt.
Cochrane Mines of Cobalt, Limited	Cochrane	Cobalt	Haileybury.
Coniagas Mines, Limited, The	Coniagas	Cobalt	Cobalt.
Crown Reserve Mining Co., Limited	Crown Reserve	Cobalt	Cobalt.
Drummond Fraction	Drummond Fraction	Cobalt	Giroux Lake.
Foster Leasing Company, Limited	Foster	Cobalt	Giroux Lake.
Hudson Bay Mines, Limited, The	Hudson Bay	Cobalt	New Liskeard.
Kerr Lake Mining Company, Limited	Kerr Lake	Cobalt	Cobalt.
La Rose Mines, Limited	La Rose	Cobalt	Cobalt.
McKinley-Darragh-Savage Mines of Cobalt, Limited	McKinley-Darragh-Savage	Cobalt	Cobalt.
Mann Mines, Limited	Mann	Gowganda	Gowganda.
Millerett Silver Mining Company, Limited	Millerett	Gowganda	Gowganda.
Nipissing Mining Company, Limited	Nipissing	Cobalt	Cobalt.
O'Brien, M.J	O'Brien	Cobalt	Cobalt.
O'Brien, M.J	Miller Lake-O'Brien	Gowganda	Gowganda.
Penn-Canadian Mines, Limited	Penn-Canadian.	Cobalt	Cobalt.
Peterson Lake Silver-Cobalt Mining Co., Limited	Peterson Lake	Cobalt	Cobalt.
Right of Way Mines, Limited, The	Right-of-Way	Cobalt	Cobalt.
Seneca-Superior Silver Mines, Limited	Seneca-Superior	Cobalt	Cobalt.
Temiskaming Mining Company, Limited	Temiskaming	Cobalt	Cobalt.
Trethewey Silver-Cobalt Mine, Limited	Trethewey	Cobalt	Cobalt.
Wettlaufer-Lorrain Silver Mines, Limited	Wettlaufer-Lorrain	Lorrain Township	Silver Centre.
Non-Producing:			
Canadian Gold and Silver Mining Co., Limited	....	....	....
Cobalt Provincial Mines, Limited	Provincial	Cobalt	Giroux Lake.
Colonial Mining Co., Limited	Colonial	Cobalt	Cobalt.
East Dome Mines, Limited	....	Cobalt	Cobalt.
Lumsden Mining Co., Limited, The	Lumsden	Cobalt	75 Sparks St., Ottawa.
York-Ontario Silver Mines, Limited	York-Ontario	Cobalt	2984 Main Street, Buffalo, N.Y.

* Now The Mining Corporation of Canada, Limited.

New Liskeard T.&N.O. station

Not only has the war in Europe ended the sale of Cobalt's silver for coinage but it has already shaken the personal lives of many local men. Unexpectedly the Germans have advanced quickly through Belgium and only now has allied resistance held them at Ypres. But more men must urgently reinforce the furious defensive. Louis Pilkington of the *Speaker* office in New Liskeard has a letter from his brother Alfred who with other Temiskaming volunteers began boarding troop ships at Quebec City on September 26. On October 3, thirty-two vessels carrying 33,000 men, 7,000 horses, motors, wagons and other equipment sailed down the St. Lawrence for Plymouth, England. Choosing to wear the kilts of the Hamilton Highlanders rather than the tight uniform of a Quebec regiment, Alfred writes that "next week [he] will probably be marching through France to assist the army under General French." From his recruiting station in the Armory built last year in Haileybury, Lieutenant Peter Ferguson has led the 97th Regiment's militiamen of the Algonquin Rifles, including Alfred Pilkington, to Valcartier camp, sixteen miles from Quebec City. Captain Robert Robinson and Lieutenant Albert Morgan are training other militia recruits in New Liskeard. While Captain J.D. Glover and Lieutenant W.F. Petermann are doing the same in Cobalt. So successful is the recruitment campaign, the Cobalt Hockey League has had to suspend this season's games. Even the O'Brien team which won last year has too few players left.

Two of the first local men to join the army at Haileybury's recruiting station in October are Jonas and Alfred Seed of Bucke township. Their father Arthur had come out from England several years ago and taken up farm homesteads in the names of each of his sons. Now the family feels its loyalty to Britain. So do the three Atkinson brothers, James, Frank and Stephen. Veterans of the Boer War they volunteer to give up their West Road farm in Firstbrook township for the sake of "God, King and Country". Unfit with a heart murmur, their Magistrate brother Siegfried never could enlist but their sisters, Hilda, Phoebe and Thyra, along with their mother living in England might be in danger from enemy attack. So does Bill Wright, another Boer War veteran, answer the call to enlist. On August 14 Bill had stepped on to the dock at Liverpool, England, to join his old Hussars' regiment. Then after his offer was declined because "he had already done his bit", he quickly returned to Haileybury where today he lies in bed painfully recuperating from a fall aboard ship. Legally secure are his Kirkland Lake claims where the Cartwright option works from a small headframe and shaft.

Valcartier Camp

Soldiers embarking, behind Haileybury's Ferguson Avenue Public School

Weary of wine, women and fuzzier songs after spending the $7,500 he received for selling his 150,000 Teck-Hughes' shares to Buffalo, New York, investors, Sandy McIntyre successfully enlists. Having changed his Scottish name of Alexander Oliphant to hide from his wife in the wilds of Canada, Sandy no longer fears slipping the disguise.

At top of Main Street on Haileybury T.&N.O. station ground

Too old to join the army at age fifty-one, Dr. Codd decides after twenty-five years in Canada to leave Haileybury and return to England. Although wife Nellie and daughter Dorothy do not share the belief he can best serve overseas, Dr. Codd leaves his house, possessions and medical practice at 18 Meridian Avenue in the care of Dr. Hector Joyal. Married this year to Florestine Laframboise of North Cobalt, Dr. Joyal needs a house but neither he nor his wife can believe this inheritance of silverware, china, crystal, tables, chairs, rugs and beds. Yet, while he continues attending Providence Hospital Dr. Joyal may also inherit treating a nun for smallpox as Dr. Codd once did. At first overwhelmed by his sole charge of all the hospital patients he soon walks with a lighter step after Dr. Walter Clifford Arnold offers to help.

Although he has just arrived in Haileybury himself, twenty-nine year old Dr. Arnold has had three years of medical experience. Two years ago he had first come north to assist Cobalt's Dr. J.A. Kane, but after suffering typhoid fever he returned to Toronto. Up till then however, he had believed his life was charmed. As a boy of fourteen he had left the family farm at Zephyr to ride as a cowboy with his Thompson relatives in Montana. Unsettled in a saddle he ventured further west to San Francisco where idle without a job he began to sort out his belongings. Then for the first time he

Dr. Henry Robinson Codd, wife Nellie, daughter Dorothy, Meridian Avenue, Haileybury, 1914

saw an old Bible his mother had placed at the bottom of the bag. And as he turned its pages a five dollar bill fell out. Enough for railway fare back to Ontario. Being the most bookish of his seven younger brothers and sisters he went to Albert College in Belleville from where, after completing four years study in two, his aunt decided again he should continue on to the University of Toronto. Taking his first medical job as a doctor on a C.P.R. ship sailing out of Quebec City, he changed his mind at the last minute. The ship sank. Starting private practice in the middle of a smallpox epidemic at Coldwater, Ontario, he found himself immune to the disease. But not next at Cobalt where he was left with a permanent hearing loss from the typhoid attack. Yet now he is back north with Dr. Jackson who needs autumn and winter relief from Haileybury practice. And if his smallpox immunity still holds, he can help Dr. Joyal whenever necessary.

Even though he joined the local militia in late August, Tom Magladery must keep serving as Temiskaming's member of the provincial legislature. And also as last year's president of New Liskeard curling club he must chair an October 26 meeting to elect officers for the coming winter when honourary president Donald McCosh will support newly chosen president Frank Haynes. Miles Binkley becomes vice president and Sam Ritchie the secretary-treasurer. Then the executive committee of Angus McKelvie, Bill Magladery and Murdie McLeod suggests keeping membership fees at eight dollars but again charging outside members only five. After they find a suitable caretaker, flooding can begin for ice as early as possible in December when they will meet once more to choose skips and rinks.

On Thursday, November 3, the day after the latest company of local militia recruits leaves for additional training at Valcartier, Quebec, Temiskaming's Children's Aid Society conducts its annual meeting at New Liskeard library. President E.C. Kingswell, treasurer George T. Smith and secretary Neil McAulay declare business as usual. Also the inspector of district foster homes, Mayor McAulay of Haileybury emphasizes sixty-two children are in the Society's care; and besides attending fifty-seven police cases in which minors have faced Judge of the juvenile court Siegfried Atkinson, he has had to issue one hundred warnings to abusive parents or guardians. Maybe some of them can blame unemployment despair but none of them, as yet, can use shell-shocked nerves as an excuse.

Gunfire does kill a local man though, for on Saturday, William Alfred Reamsbottom of Haileybury is shot in a hunting accident and dies on Sunday. Down Lake Temiskaming he had gone in Fred Sullivan's launch with Bill Shillington, Evans McCuaig and Stod Forneri to Silver Centre Landing where he kept foxes penned halfway up the road to Loon Lake. (He had penned them in Haileybury behind his LakeShore Road house until their odour finally forced a move.) Near Oxbow Lake the hunters saw a deer. By the time their gunsmoke cleared, Reamsbottom lay wounded. Although Pete Larocque, who tended the fox farm teamed his bleeding body to Silver Centre wharf and Sullivan's motorboat sped back to Haileybury hospital, Bill Reamsbottom died next morning.

Three weeks later on November 25 another death shocks the pioneer people of Temiskaming. For at three o'clock this Wednesday afternoon, sixty-three year old Charles Cobbold Farr dies of the throat cancer he has suffered for a year. This visionary founder of Haileybury, tireless promoter of Temiskaming, stubborn defender of his own ideas lived to see the accidental discovery of Cobalt's silver so discolour his feudal vision of New Ontario he often longed for the natural simplicity of fur trading times. Gone now are the deep set blue eyes beneath bushy eyebrows, the drooping moustache, the slimly bent rumpled figure shambling up Browning Street in late afternoon with O'Dawg at his heels and an eel, he had paid some local boy twenty-five cents to fish out of the lake, dangling from his hand. From the lookout perched on top of his grand three-storey house west of the railway tracks beside the pond which ancient canoes once crossed along the Matabanick trail, he would often gaze towards Lake Temiskaming where in 1874 he first travelled north labouring to survey the boundary between Ontario and Quebec. He often remembered the 1905 day he and *Habitant* poet, Dr. William Henry Drummond, sat on the front porch of his original homestead house on Main Street watching the start of a thunderstorm;

The wind struck the lake turning what had been a mirror of glass into a sheet of deep indigo. The surface was fretted with little white horses and a pall of heavy grey mist hung behind it. The storm was not long in coming. It burst upon us and the lightning flashed, the thunder roared, the wind whistled and the rain came down in sheets.

A few minutes later the thunder instead of roaring seemed to crack with the rending sound that tells of the nearness of the electric current. My house stands in an exposed position on the top of the hill overlooking the lake and is without shelter, so we had the full benefit of the storm. The Doctor was evidently not accustomed to such a display.

"Isn't it splendid!" I shouted through the deafening rattle. 'I love the lightning; it is harmless enough and there is nothing to fear.'

Hardly had the words left my lips when a second crash rent the sky overhead. It was like a blow from a sledge-hammer and was accompanied by a dazzling blinding flash of light.

Sometimes wrong but never fearful C.C. Farr survived the years. And now at the 1:30 o'clock Sunday afternoon funeral from his Browning Street home pallbearers Mayor McAulay, Robert Shillington, Fred Day, Herbert Day, Sheriff George Caldbick and Bucke township Reeve John Westron will carry his coffin to the waiting hearse for a final trip to the cemetery beside Mill Creek where he once operated Haileybury's first saw and grist mill industry.

Next evening as Haileybury curlers meet to organize their winter games, they give a moment's silence to the loss of a town legend. And the "Gang" at the Matabanick Hotel has lost one of its most loyal members. Even Harry Oakes, who plans to spend part of a gentler winter at John Weedon's boarding house while curling and raising money for his Kirkland Lake mine, has had a nodding acquaintance with C.C. Farr. And clubhouse members Lorne Herbert, Howard Dunbar, Alof Carlson, George Bagshaw, Wes Gordon, Duncan Sutherland, Evans McCuaig, John Stitt, Bob Budd, Bob Lyman, Cliff Moore, Lorne Ferguson, Herb Pickard, J. Gowd, Phil Montgomery, Joe Wesley, Taylor Pipe, Joe Branchaud, O.J. Thorpe and Fred Thompson have first-hand or affectionate hearsay stories to tell. John Stitt and George Bagshaw do try to talk of their latest gold claims in Grenfell township, four miles northwest of Kenogami station. With partners Jim Fraser, former curling club manager Silas Cook and Isabel Graham holding her late lawyer husband's share, they directed Silas' men last month to break open the veins. Down to sixteen feet in one of the slashes, the men are now sinking a shaft. Yet how many such prospecting stories have been told before? Be quiet and listen instead to the one-of-a-kind life of C.C. Farr, the members insist.

Yet in less than a week's time at the annual Saturday night meeting of neighbouring New Liskeard's Skating Rink Company not a mention is made of his name. Newly elected directors W.A. Taylor, A.E. Stephenson, M.G. Hansman, T.E. Armstrong, A. Jewell, F. Thompson and A.J. Coombe choose William Taylor as president and Allie Stephenson vice president. And after he promises to begin ice making "when weather permits.", they confirm the appointment of Eric McEwen as rink manager.

How can anyone forget, though, with furniture finally moved into the Haileybury courthouse on Tuesday that Farr's log homestead originally occupied this site? But difficult it is, perhaps, to remember, especially after roaming through the large rooms finished in oak. Go up the central stairway to Judge Hartman's office, first door to the right. Directly opposite across the hall is Police Magistrate Atkinson. Downstairs, behind the first door to the right of the front entrance is Sheriff Caldbick. Left of the entrance is Crown Attorney Smiley whose door faces that of Division Court Clerk Paul

Cobbold. Local Master of Titles W.H. Lewis has his office in the separate registry building a few feet north. Two judicial men from New Liskeard, two from Haileybury and two from Cobalt occupy the courthouse. George Caldbick and W.H. Lewis may live in Haileybury today but respectively worked in Cobalt as Provincial Police Constable and as one of the Ottawa founders of City of Cobalt Mine. A fair pacifying balance of judicial appointments from Temiskamings' three oldest towns? Morley Pumaville did not think so a year ago, when he learned Siegfried Atkinson's district appointment would eventually end his own role as New Liskeard's police magistrate. And furthermore, why was Haileybury's Tom Meagher, mining recorder George T. Smith's brother-in-law, moved from that town's mining recorder's office to become court registrar? Without anyone else asked to apply for the position.

* * *

In early 1915 the European War is digging into two opposed trenches of soldiers separated by barbed wire and artillery barrages blasting the land between into muddy pools of drowning water. Recruiting for the Borden Armoured Light battery during the week of January 15, Major Eddie Holland reveals his command of sixty men will have seven armoured cars, one semi-armoured car, six motorcycles and a combination machine shop-ammunition-transport car. Four men and an officer will man each armoured car. Captain Robert S. Robinson of New Liskeard is commanding the First Canadian Cyclist Battalion. Captain G.W. Dixon, Cobalt's mapmaker, is leading a battalion of army engineers.

Camp Borden army training camp

Not yet, though, are local soldiers precision marching over the flat surface of town skating rinks. For most townspeople the war is still too far away to consider dangerous. And on Tuesday evening, January 19, more than a hundred different costumes twirl around the ice during New Liskeard's Fancy Dress Carnival. Just as amused at guessing identities is the crowd of spectators sitting safely behind the side boards. After the last of the three-legged racers collapses at centre ice everyone shrieks with laughter as costume-bundled bodies twist through swaying barrels suspended two and a half feet above.

New Liskeard Wharf, January 22, 1915

Next Monday, however, everyone attending the 1:30 afternoon meeting in New Liskeard's Library Hall listens seriously to F.C. Hart, director of co-operators and markets, from Toronto explain how to organize a co-operative creamery. Even those farmers who have to stand at the back of the hall try to catch his every word. They best know the loss of a season's grain crop is less severely felt when cushioned by extra income from dairy produce. Yet they also know the more immediate loss of Tom Magladery to army enlistment has weakened their chance of persuading Queen's Park to build a Temiskaming creamery. On February 1, the Temiscaming Telephone Company can appoint Ferguson Hutchinson to replace Magladery as company director but local farmers despair of finding a replacement M.P.P. so closely tied in business awareness to the New Liskeard-Earlton-Englehart farming area.

Local farmers confess, though, their self interest will not help win the war. And more and more of them join long enlistment queues as recruitment teams scour northern Ontario. Prospectors Sandy McIntyre and Fred Thompson have already joined Eddie Holland's Borden Battery. Don Russell of Cobalt has joined the Royal Air Force. Percy Dunbar of Haileybury has marched off with the 48th Highlanders. And Bill Wright is well enough now to join the Canadian Army.

Wabi Iron Works is doing its wartime duty. Producing shrapnel for artillery shells, women in the pattern shop are operating the battery of presses twenty-four hours a day, seven days a week.

Reasoning its own war effort would be better spent concentrating on the Cobalt silver operation, Nipissing Mines, on March 1, cancels its Teck-Hughes' option at Kirkland Lake. An easy decision with Teck-Hughes' assays so lean in gold and the Nipissing company so short of miners in Cobalt. Certainly Nipissing needs skilled machinemen to drift and stope its Meyer Vein which still supplies vast amounts of lowgrade ore hoisted up the 4th of July shaft and carried a mile by aerial tramway across Cobalt Lake to the forty-stamp mill sloping down the hillside. Just as Savage Mine ore moves by aerial buckets to the McKinley-Darragh Mill.

Mill dumps, Savage Mine

With too many gold fines lost in the mill tailings, the Tough-Oakes company is adding a cyanide plant to its Kirkland Lake concentrator. For years the O'Brien and Buffalo mills at Cobalt have proven how profitable this final recovery method is. And with gold worth twenty dollars an ounce compared to Cobalt's silver ore at forty-six cents, how can Tough-Oakes hesitate?

At Timmins, John Bickell does not hesitate after Albert Freeman finally surrenders the presidency of McIntyre Porcupine Mines. Immediately Bickell appoints his Trethewey Silver Mine partner from Cobalt, Alex Hay, to the position. Sir Henry Pellatt who sought the job for himself must accept the vice-presidency. Although president of Mining Corporation of Canada's group of mines at Cobalt he had hoped to fatten his flow of earnings into the dream "Casa Loma" castle he is building in Toronto. But Colonel Hay better understands McIntyre manager Dick Ennis' plea: the company must spend any profits on buying the encircling Jupiter, Pearl Lake, Plenaurum and Platt Vet properties into which McIntyre's best ore bodies strike.

Aerial tramway to Nipissing Mill, Cobalt - OA - 15808-R5

Jim McRae, who spent his twentieth birthday alone in 1909 near Sandy McIntyre's bush-disguised Porcupine claim, now interviews Colonel Hay at his Haileybury home. Since Trethewey Mine owns a large amount of McIntyre stock a natural step it was for him to become president, Hay says. Especially since February 28 when Trethewey Mine closed its Cobalt operation until the price of silver improves—no sense wasting money that can strengthen McIntyre. Recently hired as editor of *Cobalt Nugget's* weekly *Mining Review*, Jim McRae fumbles his interview notes for Friday's feature article as the trolley car jerks back to Cobalt. Nipissing Central conductor Dan Murray apologizes, this is Dick Richardson's first run as motorman.

McRae has replaced editor Ben Hughes who quit in March to become Ernie Hand's partner. Together they plan a weekly publication devoted to technical mining. Using the equipment he had bought from Arthur Roebuck, a few months ago, Ernie has already begun publishing the weekly *Cobalt Press*. Yet he cannot match sales of the established *New Liskeard Speaker* or *Haileyburian*. And too expensive his operation has been: composing the newspaper in the Wallace Block basement, where the Opera House formerly stood on Cobalt Square, he has relied on two girls handsetting the copy, then sending it by streetcar to New Liskeard for final printing. One of the girls has also acted as secretary and accountant. Now with Ben Hughes' editorial skills and their newly titled *Northern Miner*'s printing press moved to a basement office in Bilsky's Royal Exchange building they will avoid bankrupting competition by narrowing news coverage to detailed mining stories other local papers mostly neglect.

On May 13, the *Haileyburian* carries a small notice that Dr. Henry Robinson Codd now living in Nunney, Somerset, England, yesterday sold his Meridian Avenue house and lots for $4,500 to Bishop E.A. Latulipe. Converted seven years ago to Roman Catholicism Dr. Codd had promised the sale if he and his family chose to stay in England. The *Haileyburian* also reports veterinary surgeon Crawford McCleary has sold his Main Street livery stable to Wilbur Scharfe and Jim McTavish. Dr. McCleary is moving to Iroquois Falls as "horse man" for Abitibi Power and Paper Company. Ludger Gagnon will become veterinary surgeon for Scharfe and McTavish.

97th REGIMENT (ALGONQUIN RIFLES.)

Unbrigaded.

2nd Divisional Area.

(Organized G. O. July, 00).

Regimental Headquarters—Sudbury, Ont.

1st Battalion (8 Companies).

Company Headquarters.

A Co.—Cobalt.
B Co.—Sudbury.
C Co.—Thessalon.
D Co.—Elk Lake.
E Co.—Cochrane.
F Co.—Haileybury.
G Co.—North Bay.
H Co.—New Liskeard.

Honorary Lieutenant-Colonel—Dyment, A. E., 14 Feb., 07.

Lieut-Colonel.

McKee, H E	17 Mar 09 (*ext'd* 31 Dec 15)

Majors (2).

Cressey, W J	28 Feb 13

Captains (8).

h ⚔ *Robinson, R S* (E)	6 Mar 12
b *McKessock*, R R (E)	24 June 12
d *Daniels, A M* (E)	24 Apr 13
Handley, J (*sm*) (E)	11 Aug 13
a *Glover, J D* (E)	18 Apr 14
c Armstrong, E F	15 Feb 15

Lieutenants (16).

Young, W H (*s s*)	27 June 07
h *Morgan, A N* (E)	17 Sept 08
e Robb, J M	8 June 10
h Taylor, A T H	17 June 10
f *Ferguson, P G* (E)	30 June 11
g Brady, G R	30 June 11
c Rothera, C F	30 June 11
a *Petermann, W F* (E)	17 June 12
d Ansley, A. J	15 June 13
	22 June 06
c Titus, E B (*s m*)	28 Sept 14
	10 Nov 13
Rogers, R P (*r m c*)	1 Jan 15 (*capt* 15 Jan 95)
d *Skill, A T	26 May 10
b *Baycroft, W C	1 Jan 13
g *Hough, W M	1 June 14
d **McKee, N F* (E)	29 Jan 14
h *Magladery, T	29 Aug 14
f *Green, C C	2 Sept 14
a *May, W T	8 Dec 14
b **Hall, R H*	1 Aug 14
e **Reade, G G H*	10 Aug 14
d **Haldane, A J*	5 Sept 14
**Stevenson, R W*	24 Sept 14
**Foster, C A*	26 Oct 14
Price, H J	28 Oct 14
a **Slaght, A G*	8 Dec 14
g **Tretheway, W R*	13 Feb 15
c **Ansley, F C R*	14 Feb 15
h **Clapperton, G*	16 Feb 15
b **Piercy, H H*	12 Mar 15

Adjutant.

Rogers, R P *lt* (*rmc*)	1 Jan 15

Instructor of Musketry.

Handley, J *capt* (*s m*)	28 Feb 14

Signalling Officer.

Young, W H *lt* (*s s*)	2 May 10

Quartermaster.

Ansley, J J	13 Feb 01 (*hon maj* 13 Feb 11)

Medical Officer.

Arthur, R H	27 Apr 01 (*maj* 29 June 06)
Cockburn, G L capt, AMC (E)	7 Oct 11
Colbeck, O W lt AMC	26 Feb 15

Chaplain.

....

CORPS RESERVE.

2nd Battalion.

Majors (2).

....

Captains (8).

....

Lieutenants (16).

Johnston, G W	15 May 10
	20 Apr 04
Lidstone, J	11 Aug 13
	28 May 10
Wallace, C C	6 Apr 14
	30 June 11

The *New Liskeard Speaker* reports the opening of Sam Eplett's Ice Cream parlour. Last year Sam and his namesake son returned to town from Coldwater village, in Medonte township. Son Gordon has now joined them to manage the plant in the Opera House basement. Manager Ernie Frisby, who two years ago bought the building then leased it for a steady profit to the Amalgamated Picture Show Company, has rented them some space beside the large furnace room. Above the stairway entrance alongside Armstrong Street, this summer's perspiring townspeople will read a sign for Eplett's Ice Cream and step down to buy a five cent cone. And already Ernie Frisby has calculated the rental income could even pay for heating the whole building next winter. And the ice cream attraction might even lure bowlers from the popular lanes across Armstrong Street, between Greenwood's store and the Windsor Hotel, to Opera House movies.

Eplett's Ice Cream factory, Grand Opera House, New Liskeard

Almost social and personal in tone, Rev. J.R. Urquhart, secretary of the Temiskaming Ministerial Association has told the *Speaker* reporter of Monday's May 10 evening dinner banquet meeting at Mrs. Stitt's house in Haileybury. After the members and their wives finished the meal, Rev. A.H. Barker of New Liskeard spoke of how he looked forward to the start of next fall's meetings. Then approving the previous minutes the members and their wives listened to Professor John Sharp read his paper on "Browning's Treatment of the Problem of Evil". His wife Ruth sat by his side.

Announcing such a problem of evil on May 28, the *Speaker* paints a black band across the top of its front page. Four days ago Lieutenant Albert Norton Morgan was killed in France. A longtime New Liskeard lawyer, director and solicitor for Temiscaming Telephone Company, who had also first formed the local militia in 1908, his death shocks New Liskeard to war's crude meaning. His father Henry Morgan of Montreal, had always hoped this son would inherit the family business. Tom McCamus, however, well knew Albert Morgan's independent bent and to console his wife and children left alone in New Liskeard, he has the telephone company write its "profound sorrow and regret."

Presbyterian church picnic, New Liskeard
At viewers left: Wes McKnight, ____, Mrs. McKnight,
Rev. Urquhart, Mrs. Urguhart, ____, ____, ____,

Obeying an appeal from Lieutenant Tom Magladery, his brother Bill and Board of Trade president C.H. Fullerton canvas' New Liskeard on Saturday, June 5, raising $500 to equip an army field kitchen. When soldiers of the 97th finally arrive at the battle line, Tom has written from training camp, only such a mobile cooking kitchen can feed them hot meals in the trenches at any time of the fighting day.

Untouched by war, gold mining at Kirkland Lake's remote bush location sputters on. Yet, in June, Arthur Cockeram's prospecting syndicate from Haileybury rejoices over a High Court decision awarding them the seven acre fraction overstaked by Bill Wright. And immediately the Connell brothers, Shirley Cragg and Cockeram accept Lake Shore Mine's offer of $30,000 cash and 50,000 shares for the lake covered sliver. Bill Wright does not consider the court decision a complete defeat, though, for he also accepts 200,000 Lake Shore shares for his forty acre claim adjoining west.

Last year Ed Horne of New Liskeard pocketed cash for his forty acres directly south of Wright's other claim at the eastern edge of the lake. Another Haileybury syndicate headed by Union Bank manager George Bagshaw and the surveying firm of Routley and Summers had then foreseen the need for a planned townsite at Kirkland Lake. And what better place than Horne's claim along the summer bush trail miners were stamping hard between the Teck-Hughes' and Tough-Oakes' operations.

More than satisfied last summer was Ed Horne when the sale money gave him enough of a grubstake to paddle back to Tremoy Lake in northwestern Quebec, after a three year's absence. Persuading skilled bushmen Bert Armstrong and Bert McDonell to accompany him he took another look at the fractured rhyolite rock, so like Kirkland Lake's. Yet, instead of rousing curiosity at the Mining Recorder's office at Ville Marie, he left the ground unstaked. But he did bring samples back for quiet assays at Davey John's inconspicuous office in Haileybury.

Ville Marie dock

On Horne's return this summer from Quebec he might not have been able to keep the trip a secret. Especially on July 1 when James Fitzpatrick hosts a huge party at Dawson's Point on Lake Temiskaming. After selling the Nipissing Central Railway he bought the Harris township farm, built a home there two years ago and added sheds, barns and a standpipe for his own private waterworks. Now with a large dance pavilion connected by boardwalk to a government wharf he has chartered the *Meteor* and *Silverland* steamers to bring whatever partygoers wish to come from New Liskeard, Haileybury and Cobalt. After this gala opening he hopes the pavilion playground will become a regular resort business on Lake Temiskaming. And a lookout point from which to guess what paddlers returning from trips to Quebec are carrying in the bottom of their canoes. Paddlers like Ed Horne.

Unable to attend Fitzpatrick's party, Routley and Summers, on July 6, have Yacht Campbell's survey crew start subdividing the Townsite claim property at Kirkland Lake. After spending the winter counting too few customers at his and Wilf Foster's store on the Teck Hughes' property following Nipissing Mines' fearful retreat from the mine option there, Yacht and his wife Maude feel their securest future rests with Routley and Summers' business firm. Especially after the firm says Yacht can remain in Kirkland Lake as sales agent for the Townsite lots.

Not feeling so secure is Howard Dunbar. On Tuesday afternoon, July 13, his Haileybury planing and woodworking factory at the top end of Main Street beside the railway tracks burns to the ground. Answering the quick call for help the fire brigade's hose wagon within a minute hustled at full speed up the hill. But the grey percherons pulled the wagon too far ahead between piles of flaming lumber. And while the firemen fought to save the horses, the flames destroyed the harness and hose. So the unhindered fire burned the rest of the lumber, sheds, factory and two box cars. Even twisting railway tracks as it leaped across the T.&N.O. right of way into lumber piles on the other side. Howard Dunbar still has a sawmill operating at Remi Lake near Moonbeam but now he must decide whether to forget the planing mill-retail business and deal only in wholesale lumber.

Dunbar Mill burns

Haileybury fire hose wagon

Down Main Street at Haileybury's Ferguson Avenue-Broadway Street corner, Phil Jory and Bert Young have no such retail business headache even though they operate the Lyric Theatre in back of their drug store block. Perched in its cage suspended from the ceiling near the store's front Ferguson Avenue door, the great green parrot will continue to command children "Buy Gum Drops"; but entering the theatre from Broadway Street, moviegoers can evade the bird's jealous squawks.

Since Ned Wright is planning to close his Haileybury bowling alley and start up the Grand Theatre, the old Theatorium and Star "nickels" on Broadway Street know their hard bench seats cannot compete much longer. George White playing the piano and his wife Maude dancing have often performed Theatorium evenings but people today are demanding silent movies. Besides showing the newest films at his Grand Theatre, Ned Wright has hired young Dick McFarlane to accompany the movies' dramatic turns on his violin. Meanwhile, Phil Jory might find his Ferguson Avenue drugstore and theatre short staffed—brother-in-law Ed Faragher who operated the ice cream parlour has joined the army.

With a wife and four young children, the youngest newly-born Frank, Ed Hargreaves, unlike his equally old brother-in-law Bill Wright, must stay to support them. And since local Haileybury building contracts will soon vanish with all manpower efforts going towards ending the war, Ed finally makes up his mind to buy Desrochers' butcher shop at the southwest corner of Main Street and Rorke Avenue, and revive the meat cutting skills he learned in England.

Ed Faragher at right, Haileybury

Finally realizing, on August 1, his Buffalo Mine at Cobalt will soon run short of dividend paying mineral ground, president Charlie Denison, haunted by his decision to drop the option on Porcupine's Dome Mine five years ago, now combines with American associates to buy the Teck-Hughes and build a fifty ton cyanide mill. With over 800 acres to mine at Cobalt,

Nipissing Mines has never felt the same anxiety to buy, and can afford not to have taken the option gamble. How much of a gamble does Denison face? Well, the Tough-Oakes is mining rich highgrade. Harry Oakes' Lake Shore Mine keeps finding lower grade deposits but anyone listening to Harry's description of a mammoth trunk treasure vein, he preaches lies under the lake, could easily be converted. And with Yacht Campbell's survey officially registered July 27, Roza Brown has already bought a lot on the townsite's central east-west street trail. Kirkland Lake might be taking permanent shape.

Be cautious, however. Remember the nearby Swastika Mining Company ran out of ore and closed down. And even though Beaver Consolidated Mine of Cobalt has paid the liquidation sale price for the fully equipped mine and pumped the underground workings dry, its miners transferred from Cobalt complain about Teck Township's barren looking rock.

To help Cobalt stay in mining shape, the T.&N.O. Commission on September 1 reduces royalties on its mineral leases from twenty-five to five percent. Threatened by cost increases and low silver prices the Mining Corporation of Canada had persuaded Arthur Cole, T.&N.O.'s resident mining engineer to appeal on their behalf. To help salvage its own mining shape Buffalo Mine has installed a new oil flotation process. Now boosted to a capacity of 500 daily tons the Buffalo mill can also re-treat its 400,000 ton mountain of tailings, estimated to contain four to seven ounces of silver per ton.

Buffalo Mine's tailings pile

As more of their mines come to rely solely on low grade milling ore and the new oil flotation method to scavenge yesterday's wastes for lost silver fines, Cobalt's mineowners must prepare for highgrade mineral futures elsewhere. The Crown Reserve operation at Kerr Lake already has its profitable Porcupine Crown Mine. Hudson Bay Mines has bought the Dome Lake Mining and Milling Company. Trethewey Mine controls McIntyre Porcupine. Buffalo Mine has just bought the Teck-Hughes. Beaver Consolidated has made a Swastika move towards Kirkland Lake. The Kerr Lake Mine is considering an option on the Smith-Labine claim at Sesekinika where surface assessment reveals promising gold veins. Now developing a gold prospect at Boston Creek the Steindler brothers' Dominion Reduction Company, formerly Nova Scotia Mine, also directs Croesus Gold Mines development of the Dobie-Leyson claim eleven miles east of Matheson in Munro township. So far only patches of gold are being found in the quartz vein there but these are spectacular. Perhaps this Matheson area so often prospected but despaired over because of heavy overburden may be worth closer examination.

On August 21, E.W. King Dodd's discovery of free gold below Howard Falls on Kowkash River, nine miles northwest of the National Transcontinental Railway, 297 miles west of Cochrane, sends over four hundred prospectors wildly staking the region. But not until next spring's meltwater has dried will Cobalt's mineowners learn whether prospectors surface pawings have bared any ground there worth buying. Yet little does Sir Henry Pellatt's Mining Corporation of Canada care. For once the 3,600 foot long, twenty inch wire-wound, wood stave pipeline finishes draining Cobalt Lake into Mill Creek, the company expects to devote all its attention to an exposed mass of silver veins. All the while at home in Cobalt.

Draining Cobalt Lake, September 2, 1915, looking east from railway embankment in front of Cobalt station

Because of Cobalt mineowners' anxious need for new mineral ground, local prospectors are prospering. In July, Pete McDonough earned a $10,000 commission for claims stake last year at Boston Creek. Brother Joe has recently received a bonus of 30,000 shares from Boston Creek's Miller-Independence Mine. And self-assured by his additional ninety dollars a month salary as fieldman for Fred Connell, Joe has started dreaming of his own future as a mineowner.

What about owning some of the new silver mining ground between Haileybury and New Liskeard? President Henry Higgins of London, England, believes in its value. In June, his Dickson Creek Mining Company manager Harry Hollands-Hurst directed picks and shovels trenching claims on lots nine and ten in concession five of Bucke township. Now out on the point of land north of the mouth of Dickson's Creek where Lake Temiskaming's cold September waters sluggishly roll, Hollands-Hurst has a twenty-five horsepower boiler powering a compressor and hoist for six miners sinking an inclined shaft.

Saturday, September 4, only a faint drilling noise reaches Nipissing Central trolley passengers from New Liskeard as they cross Dickson's Creek a few hundred feet upstream just after switching off the main line T.&N.O. track. Although easing east, the spur line section does not reach Lake Temiskaming's shore until past the oil docks at Moore's Cove. Regardless at this Labour Day time none of the trolley passengers has any desire to see the minesite— not with baseball games and horse races about to start at Farr's Park in Haileybury. Nor are they interested on the way back home. That Cobalt's LaRose baseball team defeated Ville Marie's players then batted an even larger score against the pick-up team of Haileybury and New Liskeard no longer pained them, since New Liskeard's Cliff Burkholder and Colin McRae's trotters won the most important horse races of the day.

Despite the steady decline of Cobalt's producing mines, the northern demand for graduates of Haileybury's technical mining school course is increasing. So much that Haileybury School Board has asked Nipissing Mines to prepare plans for a mining laboratory. Now Jim Denny, Jimmy Johnston and A.E. (Porkie) Flynn are designing a forty by sixty foot building with a small test mill shop and assay office. Because George Cole intends to enlist in the army, fellow teacher Flynn will be left alone to supervise construction of the mill building next year. How, he wonders, can he involve his mining school students in helping him install the equipment?

Yet Northern Ontario must equip itself for more than short-lived mines. Just beyond New Liskeard's town line, the provincial government has bought a quarter section, 160 acres of Robert West's bush farm, on the east side of the North Road. As the government's agricultural representative William G. Nixon, a graduate last year from the Ontario Agricultural College at Guelph, will supervise the development of an experimental demonstration farm here. Since arriving in New Liskeard last year to replace C.A. Galbraith, his office has become the local centre for practical advice on crops, drainage surveys, live stock and seed. New Liskeard had previously donated five acres along Niven Street where the Agricultural Hall was built. And annual seed fairs in its upper rooms and livestock judging below have stirred the pride of local farmers; but since last winter when Bill Nixon used the upstairs to teach them short courses, they testify his scientific methods have bolstered the size of their crops and cattle. Just what Howard Ferguson, Ontario's Minister of Lands, Forest and Mines, at the public meeting in the Opera House last April 22 had said would happen.

Teaching full-time this fall at Haileybury, A.E. Flynn must worry about younger high school students in his mining course, especially his best student, the son of a German miner at Cobalt. Now labelled an enemy alien, anyone with a German name or ancestor is suspected of being an enemy sympathizer or spy. Since many Anglo Saxons are refusing to enlist in the Canadian army because they accuse Germans of slyly waiting to fill their jobs, most Cobalt mineowners are refusing to hire more aliens. Mining Corporation of Canada has even declared that in November it will discharge all enemy aliens working in its Cobalt mines. Many local people also want a law passed to register all enemy aliens: do not let them hide. Yet why does an innocent son have to suffer his father's loss of a job? Flynn asks, and who can prove his father guilty of treason? But who has to? is the immediate reply: anyone born in a foreign country whose submarines could torpedoe the *Lusitania*, drowning 2,000 defenceless people, must share responsibility for murder.

Jeanette and George Hamilton, 76 LakeShore Road, Haileybury

Rather than join the army and return to Europe which he left for Cobalt five years ago or accept the label of enemy alien, Stanley Siscoe along with Joe Samulski and a few other Polish friends "has taken to the Quebec bush" settling on a small island in Lake Kienawisik, the head basin for Harricanaw River. Here, seventy-five miles east of the Ontario border, they plan to spend the war years mining a quartz vein Stanley discovered and staked last year. Of Ed Horne prospecting another lake to the west, they know nothing.

And although Rev. J.R. Urquhart of New Liskeard's St. Andrew's Presbyterian church nods hello to Ed Horne shouldering a packsack through the front door of the Grand Union Hotel on Whitewood Avenue, he also senses nothing this October 14 evening of Horne's invisible tie to Stanley Siscoe in Quebec. Tonight at The Club Rooms, Mayor Byam is presenting C.H. Fullerton with a silver tea service in farewell honour of his leaving town to become superintendent of the engineering department of Colonization of Roads at Queen's Park in Toronto. Rev. Urquhart will add the town's blessing.

Jory family, 80 LakeShore Road, Haileybury

1. John Jory
2. Emma Jory
3. Phil Jory
4. Jean Jory
5. Billy Jory

Almost two weeks later, on October 25, as honourary president of his church's Presbyterian Guild, Rev. Urquhart speaks to young adults organizing work for the coming winter. Only twenty members attend this Monday evening meeting but so enthusiastic is their choice of Miss Delta Inglis as president, Clarence Wismer as vice-president, Clifford Brown as secretary-treasurer and Miss Margaret Pelton as pianist, the church hall resounds with hand clapping cheers. Chosen to rouse more of the regular members for next month's meeting, Olga Sirr and Bertha Keeler wonder if the hall can stand much more merriment. Miss Manes will convene the devotional committee; Miss Foster, the missionary; Miss M. Brown, social and Mrs. Wismer the musical committee. Excusing himself from any talk of how he will convene his citizenship committee, Bill Nixon must leave the meeting early. Also living in Goddard's bachelor boarding house beside the Post Office on Armstrong Street with the town's newest doctor, John McCullough, who has replaced Dr. Fisher as the T.&N.O. physician, Bill has promised to guide his medical friend later tonight on an emergency trip to a sick farmer near Milberta.

Olga and Stella Sirr

Close behind the doctor's horse and buggy follows Olga Sirr. To her ice cream and confectionery store on Armstrong Street she must go to prepare for tomorrow's customers. Having just this year taken over the business from Joe McKinnery she has the monthly rent of $17.00 for W.A. Evans and the loan of $200 from her mother's brother Wes Mumford of Magnetawan to pay. With her uncle's loan she has bought a soda fountain, tables, chairs and two glass diplay cases. And her sister Stella, though more of a trained dressmaker, helps as a partner. Olga began work at Greenwood's store in 1910. Four years later she saw her own opportunity. Now eighteen years old she feels as independent as her mother Annie who has the Liberty Lodge boarding house at the northeast corner of Rebecca and Murray streets. Ever since the Sirr family arrived from Sundridge in 1905 to live with the Marsden's on Catherine Street, Olga, her sisters Vesta, Stella, Zola and Verna, her brothers Justin, Reg and Frank have watched New Liskeard grow. Now with her own business in the Evan's Block between Yates' liquor store and Bill Nixon's Department of Agriculture office, Olga believes she can help the town and herself prosper even more.

Sirr boarding house, corner of Rebecca and Murray street, New Liskeard

What has happened to Dr. Fisher? Although the *New Liskeard Speaker* says, "he has reached an age when he might very well have been relieved of such arduous work," the doctor has volunteered for service on the front battle lines in France. Appointed Captain in the Canadian Army medical corps, he will superintend the hospital staff mending wounded troops, only a few feet away from where they have fallen.

Army recruitment throughout Temiskaming peaks in December when Captain Ernest Armstrong, Cobalt's pioneer dentist, receives 97th Regiment orders to mobilize the first Algonquins now known as the 159th Canadian Battalion. Promoted to Lieutenant Colonel-in-Command, Dr. Armstrong makes Haileybury Armory his headquarters to speed up the manning of eight companies from as far west as Thessalon. Father J.R. O'Gorman of Cobalt quickly enlists as chaplain. Just turned eighteen Melvin Robb of Haileybury quits his Union Bank job and enlists as a rifleman. On Wednesday morning, December 15, George White waves goodbye to his children James and Percy at home with their mother Maude at the north end of Latchford Street and walks through galoshes deep snow to join Haileybury's F Company. With Walter Willans, whom he had persuaded into singing again, George organized a series of concerts last winter and summer in New Liskeard's Opera House, Haileybury's Armory and Cobalt's Lyric Theatre; but now he feels his piano playing skills can better boost troop morale closer to the front lines.

Haileybury Armory

Although the shortage of Temiskaming labour worsens, the silver price morale of Cobalt mineowners recovers from a September low of forty-six cents to a November high of almost fifty-two cents. Of seventeen companies shipping ore this 1915 year the Nipissing, Coniagas, Kerr Lake, Seneca Superior and Temiskaming have been most productive. Along with eight million LaRose and McKinley-Darragh ounces; concentrates from the

Nipissing, Dominion Reduction, Cobalt Reduction, Buffalo and O'Brien mills and the camp's highgrade ore, total silver shipments have amounted to almost twenty-five million ounces, down five million from last year but only slightly lower than last year's twelve million dollar market value. And the grade of ore hoisted has been better than last year's.

Sand tables, McKinley-Darragh mill

Like the other mines of Cobalt desperately aware of diminishing ore reserves, Kerr Lake Mining Company has finally decided on exploring elsewhere for new life. With a six month option on Dan Smith and Gilbert Labine's three claims in concession two of Maisonville township, about one and a quarter miles due north of Sesekinika station, the company has Albert Terrill supervising fifteen men collaring a prospect shaft on a narrow quartz vein showing free gold.

Far from its LaRose Mine beginning at Cobalt, the Timmins-McMartin Syndicate is now milling 1,500 tons of Hollinger Mine's Porcupine ore a day. And it has plans to increase the rate to a gigantic 4,000 tons.

Yet despite this Midas wealth, Noah Timmins has persuaded his partners to buy the old Wright lead mine on the Quebec shore of Lake

Temiskaming. Twenty-two years ago when he and brother Henry owned their first mineral property a few miles down the lake near Fabre, they had hoped its meagre copper showing might develop into the size of Wright's galena silver deposit. It never did. Then Wright's ore grew leaner at depth. Today, however, Noah Timmins has achieved his belated ownership dream. And his geologist's agree that Wright's old mine could be sitting on the eastward extension of Cobalt's flow of silver, reaching through Bucke township to the lake edge of Agauncio Mine, just five miles away. Certainly Lake Temiskaming fills a north-south rift fault which would have dropped ore veins in a block hundreds of vertical feet below, but where do they push upwards on the undisturbed eastern side of the fault zone?

O'Brien mine and mill, Cobalt

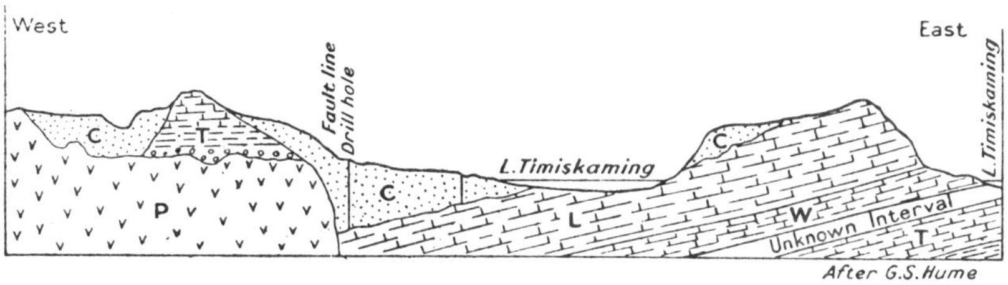

Vertical section, east and west through New Liskeard; horizontal scale 2 miles to an inch, vertical scale 800 feet to an inch. The Lake Timiskaming fault is shown at "fault line." The rocks on the east side of the fault have been faulted down 800 to 1,000 feet.

C—Post Glacial clay.
L—Lockport formation } Silurian.
W—Walsi formation }
T—Haileyburian—Ordovician.
P—Pre-Cambrian.

Today's snow, however, covers Quebec's Guiges and Duhamel townships too deeply for the Timmins brothers to explore. And the weather around Lake Temiskaming is growing colder.

Tables showing the average mean highest, mean lowest, and the mean temperature; also the highest and lowest temperature on record, and the average precipitation.

HAILEYBURY, TIMISKAMING—QUEBEC BOUNDARY.

1895-1915 (21 years).

Month.	Temperature.				Absolute.		No. days R. or S.	Rain-fall.	Snow-fall.	Total Precip.
	Mean High.	Mean Low.	Mean	Daily Range.	Max.	Min.				
January	17.4	— 4.2	6.6	21.6	48	—40	16	0.29	17.2	2.01
February	20.2	— 2.9	8.7	23.1	47	—48	12	0.20	16.0	1.80
March	31.6	8.4	20.0	23.2	71	—34	13	0.45	14.5	1.94
April	48.4	26.6	37.5	21.8	87	— 3	16	1.23	5.0	1.73
May	62.0	39.3	50.6	22.7	93	17	14	2.84	1.4	2.98
June	73.2	50.0	61.6	23.2	100	28	12	2.91	....	2.91
July	76.7	55.3	66.0	21.4	102	36	14	3.74	....	3.74
August	72.6	51.9	62.3	20.7	94	27	13	2.86	....	2.86
September	64.9	44.8	54.8	20.1	91	24	15	3.45	....	3.45
October	51.5	34.7	43.1	16.8	80	13	14	2.56	2.6	2.82
November	35.3	21.4	28.4	13.9	63	—25	15	0.99	13.9	2.38
December	22.0	4.9	13.5	17.1	51	—35	17	0.35	20.0	2.35
	....	....	....	....	....	....	....	21.91	90.6	30.97

Av. date last frost, June 5th. Av. date first frost, September 11th.

BIBLIOGRAPHY

1. Atkinson, Cyril, private memoir, 1970
2. Barnes, Michael, *Link With a Lonely Land*, Boston Mills Press, Erin, 1985
3. Cassidy, George L., *Arrow North, The Story of Temiskaming,* Temiskaming Printing, New Liskeard, 1976
4. *Cobalt Daily Nugget,* Cobalt, 1910-1915
5. Cumming, James D., *Now and Then,* Northern Miner Press, Toronto, 1966
6. *Haileyburian,* Haileybury, June 8, 1912
7. *Haileyburian,* Haileybury, July 29, 1954
8. Helm, Norman, *Tri-Town Trolleys, The Story of the Nipissing Central Railway,* Highway Book Shop, Cobalt, 1984
9. Hoffman, Arnold, *Free Gold, The Story of Canadian Mining,* Associated Book Service, New York, 1958
10. Jones, L. and Lonn, G., *Historical Highlights of Canadian Mining,* Pitt Publishing, Toronto, 1973
11. Kindle, E.D., *Gold Occurrences of Ontario East of Lake Superior,* Department of Mines, Memoir 192, King's Printer, Ottawa, 1936
12. Lebourdais, D.M., *Metals and Men,* McClelland and Stewart, Toronto, 1957
13. Lonn, George, *The Mine Finders,* Pitt Publishing, Toronto, 1966
14. McFarlane, Leslie, *A Kid in Haileybury,* Highway Book Shop, Cobalt, 1975
15. Miller, Willet G., *Cobalt-Nickel and Silver Arsenides of Temiskaming,* Ontario Bureau of Mines, 4th edition, King's Printer, Toronto, 1913
16. *New Liskeard Speaker,* New Liskeard, 1910-1915
17. Pain, S.A., *The Way North,* Ryerson Press, Toronto, 1964
18. Pain, S.A., *Three Miles of Gold,* Ryerson Press, Toronto, 1960
19. Robinson, A.H.A., *Gold in Canada,* Department of Mines, King's Printer, Ottawa, 1933
20. Smith, Phillip, *Harvest From the Rock,* MacMillan, Toronto, 1986
21. Temiskaming and Northern Ontario Railway reports, North Bay, 1910-1915
22. Todd, E.W., *Kirkland Lake Gold Area,* Ontario Department of Mines, King's Printer, Ottawa, 1933
23. Wetjen, Andre and Irvine, L.H.T., *The Kirkland Lake Story,* Highway Book Shop, Cobalt, 1988

INDEX